My New Routine
Surviving the Death of My Spouse
A to Z

By Agustus Alexander Beck, MD

Life is for the living.
Death is for the dead.
Let life be like music.
And death a note unsaid.
—Langston Hughes, *The Collected Poems*

Dedication

This book is dedicated to the love of my life, Catherine, and to my children, Declan and Violet. I will continue to do my best to care for and raise my children in hopes of becoming a better person and better father every day, while always remembering the love their mother had for them.

This book is also dedicated to anybody who has been affected by depression, postpartum depression, or suicide. Depression is a treatable illness, as is postpartum depression. The key is education, awareness, and identifying who needs help. That person could be a neighbor, a coworker, or someone who lives in your own house. That person could be someone you see everyday. That person could even live in the reflection in your own mirror. Help is out there for those who need it. Please don't ignore the problem, and please help those who need it.

Introduction

What you are about to read is a true and accurate account of my life and the events that transpired before and after my wife's death. I decided to use the writing of this book as a healing process, and if it ends up helping other people unlucky enough to have gone through a similar tragedy, all the better. The following pages are filled with topics in alphabetical but not necessarily chronological order. This was done on purpose to represent my now-unstructured life. I quickly realized that my existence turned upside down after my wife's passing, and my usually well-organized life became chaotic. I have spent the days since my wife's funeral attempting to reclaim order and sense in my life; however, that is easier said than done. Thus the ensuing sections may not flow "in order," but there is some semblance of an arrangement as the topics run alphabetically. It's sort of like my new life, trying to regain sense in my existence while surrounded by turmoil as I begin my new routine.

One final note before we move on, some brief words of caution before you proceed: I do apologize in advance if my story becomes monotonous or appears too depressing. This is an unavoidable consequence when you, in your new routine, find yourself struggling to stay afloat while trapped in your own sea of despair. It's now my unfortunate reality, and you're invited to take a look. So turn the page, and let's begin.

4:19 p.m.
September 27, 2012

That's the moment everything changed. That's when my life was forever altered. My cell phone rang as I walked out of the break room at work. I pulled my phone out and saw "Barbara" on my caller ID, and I immediately new something was wrong. Barbara is—well, was—my wife's mother. And although I think she is the greatest, she absolutely never—I mean never—called me. There had never been a reason for her to until that day, until that exact moment. Little did I know that after I answered that call, my life, my existence, my routine would change forever.

As I answered my phone, all I could hear was despair, dread, and pain on the other line. Barb was crying; she was barely audible, in fact. All I could make out was that she "found Catherine" in my closet. That's the moment I knew she was gone. It's hard to explain what's it like to have your world crash down upon you. It's even more difficult to put into words what your mind goes through when you are completely consumed with pain. That moment—in fact, that entire day—is somewhat a blur, but it's also crystal clear. I suppose it's the body's way of holding onto the pain as the mind attempts to block it out. I do remember crying out in disbelief, yet, deep down, I knew what Barb meant. She had found Catherine hanging in our bedroom closet. In plain English, she meant Catherine had committed suicide.

I dropped my cell and crumbled to the ground. I remember distinctly crying out in pain. It's sort of strange to completely lose it in a public place, surrounded by coworkers, surrounded by strangers, surrounded by patients. At that moment I had regressed. I was completely numb. My nurse, Arline, thankfully picked up my phone and continued to talk with my mother-in-law while I was stuck in a fetal position. After a minute or so, I got up, walked to another room, and proceeded to collapse on the floor yet again. All the while I continued to scream in pain.

Although I was physically OK, my mind had completely shut down. I remember lying on the floor and rocking back and forth, repeating over and over again, "I can't do this alone. I can't do this alone." To my coworkers, the complete strangers in the office, and even to myself, it appeared that I meant I could not envision taking care of my kids, my newborn twins who had recently been discharged from the hospital after being born three months prematurely. But now I realize the true meaning of my words. Subconsciously, I meant I couldn't live my life alone, that I couldn't possibly survive in this world without my partner, my wife, my best friend...

Yet here I am today, writing to tell about it.

Aftermath

Sixty minutes. That's the average commute time home from my office at the end of the day during rush hour. That's how long I was in the car driving home, alone, after just finding out my wife had hung herself in our bedroom closet.

When I look back upon that drive, it's a wonder I'm still alive. Trust me, my office staff tried to stop me as I raced out the door; they just couldn't. That whole drive home was a nightmare, worse than anything you could imagine. By that time I knew in my heart that she was dead. But there was still that hope, that sliver of a chance that I would race home and find her very sick, ill, but still alive. But deep down, I knew the truth.

I drove through a film of tears. I remember punching my steering wheel, my center console, screaming out in pain, anguish. Despair, panic, fear, misery—pick a word, crack open a thesaurus, it can't do my drive home that day proper justice. I tried to occupy my time the best I could. I remember calling my parents, my brother, my best friend, all in a panic, screaming uncontrollably, "Catherine is dead! Catherine is dead!" over and over again. It was true darkness, true pain.

But it got worse. I remember pulling up to my house and seeing five cop cars in my driveway and on the street in front of my residence. I parked my car and ran inside. A large policeman stopped me in my tracks, and I remember screaming, "Is she alive? Is she still alive?" But I knew the answer before he could even say a word. I could see the look on his face, a look I've come to know all too well these days—the look of sorrow, the look of pity. All that poor cop could muster was, "Sir, I can't say. The medics are still upstairs." But I knew, I could see it in his eyes, and I collapsed yet again. I hit the floor like a ton of bricks. I'd never really understood the expression "fetal position," but that's what I did. I fell on the floor for the third time that day and was consumed by my pain, my tears.

I'm not sure how long I was down—maybe seconds, maybe minutes. But I finally got up and proceeded to race about my house in search of my kids, not paying attention to the legions of strangers all about. Cops, medics, neighbors, random people—all standing, all staring at me like a bad reality TV show. I found my daughter, Violet, sleeping peacefully—so young, so innocent—and I broke down again. I dared not wake her up, so I searched for my son, Declan. I forget who was holding him, but I snatched him out of the person's hands and sat down on my front stairs. I remember distinctly cupping his head in my hands and crying, rocking back and forth. For the rest of my life, I'll remember that moment, crying with my son in my arms, rocking back and forth, saying over and over again, "I'm so sorry, I'm so sorry" while complete strangers watched on.

That moment has, and will always, haunt me. That's the moment darkness set in and sadness took over. That's the moment life changed, for me and both of my kids, forever.

Ain't No Sunshine

Ain't no sunshine when she's gone
It's not warm when she's away
Ain't no sunshine when she's gone
And she's always gone too long
Anytime she goes away
(Bill Withers)

Anger

Believe it or not, I'm not angry. I've heard from other people, mostly guys, that they would be angry as hell if their wife left them, alone, widowed, with newborn twins. Newborns who were sick, born early, and had spent months in the hospital.

My response to that is, you really don't know how you'd react until it happens to you, which is true, no matter how you cut it. What I've gone through, you can't relate to it, you can't just talk about it or read about it and translate the experience, the true emotions. Impossible. Unless you've lived it, I don't think you can judge it. Plus, it's just not my nature, it's not my personality. First and foremost, I believe anger is a wasted emotion, wasted energy. For other people, it might be different, and I respect that. That's their decision. But it's not how I deal with things.

Even if it was, even if I was known as Angry Guy, that emotion still wouldn't benefit me. Whom should I be angry with, really? Catherine? No, not a chance. I don't and never will blame her for what happened. You have to understand how much Catherine loved our kids. She absolutely loved them, to a fault. She was there, at the hospital, every day for months. She never took a day off, never. She loved them so much it hurt her. It pained her to see them go through what they endured, what happened to them. People say how hard it is to see their kids get hurt, or how difficult it is to watch their kids get vaccinations. Well, simple shots and vaccinations pale in comparison to what our children endured. Our kids were poked, prodded, placed on respirators, stuck in incubators, and my son even underwent heart surgery. Day after day both of my children were in the hospital. Catherine was there to support them, every morning and every afternoon, and she was there every evening with me after I got off work.

So, no, I'm not angry with Catherine. I don't blame her. The only emotion I have for her is sadness. I hurt, truly hurt. Deep down it upsets me, knowing that Catherine was in so much pain that her only outlet was suicide. It pains me to know that she was that upset, that much in despair, that full of guilt, that she chose death over life. And the guilt part tears me up. She never admitted it, but I know. I now know deep down she felt guilty about going into labor prematurely, even though it clearly wasn't her fault. There was no rational explanation for what happened to us, for her going into labor three months early. No con-crete medical reason to explain why. Sometimes sh*t happens and it's no one's fault, there's no good explanation or reason.

So, no, I'm not angry with Catherine for what she did, and I never will be. Sadness, that's all I feel when I think about what has happened. And that's what I tell people if they ask. If they feel differently, so be it. That's their opinion. But I challenge anybody to compare situations. Let me know the next time you come across a situation similar to mine, because it's fairly uncommon. Twins, born prematurely, spend three months in the hospital; one baby almost dies after surgery, and then their mother, suffering from postpartum depression, commits suicide. Yep, not too terribly common. Before you can judge someone, you have to walk in their shoes. It sounds so clichéd, but it's true. And when you do, you might see things differently; you might not. But for me, anger is not an option. I've got plenty of other things on my plate to occupy my mind. Trust me.

Bad Day

Where is the moment we needed the most?
You kick up the leaves and the magic is lost
They tell me your blue skies fade to gray
They tell me your passion's gone away
And I don't need no carryin' on

You stand in the line just to hit a new low
You're faking a smile with the coffee to go
You tell me your life's been way off-line
You're falling to pieces every time
And I don't need no carryin' on

'Cause you had a bad day, you're taking one down
You sing a sad song just to turn it around

You say you don't know, you tell me don't lie
You work on a smile and you go for a ride

You had a bad day, the camera don't lie
You're coming back down and you really don't mind
You had a bad day
You had a bad day
(Daniel Powter)

Bath Time

Bath time was always a source of both joy and frustration, more so for Catherine than me. She always had this expectation, this vision, this plan of a perfect pregnancy and perfect kids. Her vision was obviously shattered as soon as she was placed on bed rest, and she clearly never recovered. While our kids slowly got better and were both eventually discharged from the hospital, she still held onto this expectation, even though it never really coincided with reality. She wanted our kids to smile right away, she wanted them to interact with us, she wanted them to be further along in their development than they were. It bothered her terribly that they weren't. The obvious problem was their age. They were both, physically and chronologically speaking, several months old. But since our kids were born three months prematurely, their developmental age was not as old as their actual chronological age. This presented a problem, one of many that Catherine was never able to overcome. Another issue was that we had other friends, good friends, who had given birth that past summer to happy, healthy children, babies who were doing well and making progress, babies who were developing without difficulties. It's not like Catherine didn't want her friends' children to do well; it's not that at all. But it's hard on you as a parent to hear other people talk about their children when your own kids are sick and in the hospital.

When we were finally able to take our kids home, Catherine did her best to carry on. But she still had this expectation that they would immediately love bath time, that they would splash around in the water and smile. Unfortunately, her expectations could not have been further from our reality. As soon as we had our children home, the crying began. And the crying never really stopped, unless they were asleep. Nonstop. I realize that for parents of infants, this is nothing new, but for us, after months of daily hospital visits and finally bringing our kids home, our expectation was that everything would be OK. For the most part, with the twins' health and development to that point, it was. But back then, when Catherine was still alive, both of our kids absolutely hated bath time. I remember distinctly Catherine looking up at me while bathing Violet—I was holding Declan, and both kids were crying, mind you—and asking me with the saddest of eyes, "When will they smile? When will they like bath time?" All I could say was, "I don't know, but it will come. It will eventually happen."

As I write this, it's been eighty-three days since Catherine passed away, and now both of my kids enjoy bath time. They splash around, constantly smile, and actually start to cry when you take them out of the water. I see their progress, I see their development, their ability to achieve tiny milestones on a daily basis, and I get upset. I cry. Trust me, I'm happy as hell that they're doing as well as they are. But Catherine will never be able to see them grow up. She will never be able to see them develop and achieve these milestones. She will never see how well they're doing, how wonderful they are. She won't be able to hear them speak their first words, watch them crawl, or chase after them when they start to run.

I think about this when it's bath time. I go over this a million times when I see them, and it hurts. But I carry on, because in the end, Catherine wanted the world for our kids. I realize that it's up to me to take care of them, to bathe them, to teach them, to care for them as best I can. Because that's what Catherine would be doing right now if she were with us, with me and our kids.

Bed Rest

That's when everything changed. That's the moment our lives were turned upside down. At least it was before it really went sideways later on. Sometimes you can pinpoint the time or event that totally changes everything. And that was it. Catherine was never the same after she was put on bed rest. Never.

It was mid-April 2012. She had begun experiencing contractions. Now, mind you, she was only five months pregnant at this time. So we both knew the gravity of the situation. Especially Catherine. She clearly understood that going into premature labor at five months pregnant with twins was not a small problem. It was a big f*cking problem. And she was never the same.

She stayed in our bedroom on strict bed rest for almost three weeks. It was terrible. Miserable. At that time, I thought it was the worst. Little did I know, true misery would only follow and follow and follow for the next several months leading up to and not exclusive to Catherine's death.

Back then I would come home every day from work and immediately go upstairs. I would always find Catherine lying in our bed, several water bottles next her and one in her hand. The only recommended therapy for her was to "stay hydrated." So that's what Catherine did. All day and all night, she constantly drank water. She was the most hydrated person on this planet, rest assured. In the end, all that hydration, all that water, didn't change anything.

The worst thing was the look on her face, the look in her eyes. The fear, the complete look of terror. It was hard to take, and I did my best to reassure her. I spoke my fair share of "Oh, everything will be all right. It'll be OK." And it wasn't just lip service at the time. Back then, in the spring of 2012, I really did believe everything was going to be OK. Honestly. I can't explain why I felt that way, and obviously, in retrospect, I was terribly wrong. But back then, I was optimistic.

But Catherine wasn't that optimistic. Somehow, someway, she knew. Call it mother's instinct or just plain intuition, but Catherine knew something terrible was going to happen. She knew that everything was not going to be OK. I now look back upon that time and shake my head. I think of the time she spent on bed rest and I can't help myself from crying. I remember how scared she was back then, how terrified she was about going into premature labor. I remember her eyes. Her beautiful light blue eyes, so innocent, so scared—and with the look of guilt. I believe she blamed herself, although she had no reason to. She didn't smoke, didn't drink, didn't consume caffeine, didn't eat sushi or lunchmeat. She played the entire pregnancy by the book, by the pregnancy bible. She took her prenatal vitamins, went to her doctor's appointments, and on and on and on. She was a model citizen, perfect in every way. Yet I knew she blamed herself for going into premature labor.

As the days went by, I would come home from work, refill her water bottles, make dinner, and bring it upstairs to eat in our bedroom. And that was our new routine. Well, at least it was until true darkness set in. Until it got worse. Until she was admitted to the hospital. That's when it truly fell apart. That's when our lives, our entire existence, became unglued. There was no turning back at that point. That's when my routine changed forever.

Bees

Catherine was one of the strongest, most confident individuals I have ever met, one of the million qualities that drew me to her. She was also fearless, to a point. She did have one phobia, one irrational fear. She was scared to death of bees, which I always found a little amusing because I don't have any real phobias. This doesn't make me a better person, but it did make it more difficult for me to understand her strong fear of bees. She wasn't even technically allergic to bees. In fact, she had never been stung by a bee, which was why I thought her phobia was amusing. She was just convinced, for some irrational reason, that she was allergic to bees.

On the rare occasion we would happen to see a bee, she would scream and run in the opposite direction. She would then promptly ask me to write her a prescription for an EpiPen, which is a miniature "antidote" people who are legitimately allergic to bees carry in their pocket for emergency situations. I, of course, would always brush her off and ask, "How do you even know you're allergic to bees?" She would just look at me and say, "I know. I just know."

I'm not really sure why I am bringing this up now. It's just one of the random memories I hold onto since Catherine passed away. It seems that my mind wanders these days, and I can't always control where my thoughts travel. A lot of the time, I focus on the pain and emptiness. But sometimes, if I'm lucky, I remember her smile, her wonderful personality, and all the moments we shared over the course of our life together, some big, some small. I think it's the small moments that, when put together, make up the life we eventually built for ourselves. I am trying to hold onto those moments, right or wrong, because I miss her. I truly miss her—and I even miss her irrational fear of bees (apiphobia).

Bereavement

Definition: (noun) Also known as grief, a multifaceted response to loss, particularly to the loss of someone or something to which a bond has formed.

Now that we have established the definition, let me tell you what I think bereavement is. It's pain, plain and simple. Emotional and mental pain, which, if you let it get out of hand, can cause physical pain. I found that out the hard way. The first seventy-two hours after Catherine passed away, I was so distraught that I couldn't eat anything. I basically drank coffee and a little bit of water. That was it. I literally didn't eat anything. I really wasn't hungry. I had no desire to eat—and little desire to live.

It's sort of odd, not eating. If you think about it, it really is amazing how much of the day you spend thinking about food—what your next meal will be, what you plan on eating for breakfast, for lunch, for dinner, for a snack. That was thrown out the window after Catherine died. I had absolutely no interest in food for almost three weeks. All told, I ended up losing almost twenty pounds, which is a decent amount of weight when you weigh less than one hundred fifty pounds soaking wet.

After I had a bad experience with leg cramps from lack of eating, I slowly starting consuming some calories. For some reason, I was always a little nauseated, and the thought of eating much of anything made it that much worse. The only thing I could stomach was soup. Nothing solid. And it was not from lack of opportunity, because I was constantly surrounded by a sea of food. It's true what they say. When someone dies, people do bring food. After living through that experience, I find it a little odd. But I understand. My house was constantly full of people—friends, relatives, and in-laws. And having food around was definitely helpful because there were a whole lot of mouths to feed. The last thing I wanted to do was cook. So I do have to admit it was beneficial. However, I wanted no part of it. I had no interest in eating.

Now, my lack of eating didn't last forever, which is a good thing because I was really starting to waste away. I eventually started to eat for the people around me, not for myself. Everybody was really concerned about me, and I couldn't blame them. All day my friends and family would ask, "What do you want to eat? What can I fix you to eat?" I could see the scared look in their eyes, and I didn't want to hurt my family with my own pain and suffering. It wasn't fair. I didn't want people to baby-sit me on top of dealing with the loss of Catherine. So one day I forced myself to eat a sandwich. I basically told myself to suck it up and eat something. It didn't really go that well, but thankfully I didn't refund anything. I didn't throw up.

From there I slowly started eating solids. I didn't really care what I ate. I was basically treating myself like a machine, filling myself up with fuel, just enough to function and carry on with my day. It really took several months for me to start actually eating food again on a regular basis. But it's still not the same. Well, nothing really is. It's hard to explain, but I don't really enjoy food like I used to, which is not saying much, because besides my kids, I don't really enjoy much of anything anymore.

People say that this is part of the grieving process and that things will get better. But I doubt it, I really do. From where I'm sitting, things will always be different. Because I'm a different person now. Bereavement isn't just a multifaceted response to a loss, like the definition says. It's also not just a lack of appetite or weight loss. It's also not just visiting the cemetery several times a week so you can see your dead wife's gravesite. It's more than that. It really does change you, at least it did me. It's hard to explain unless you've experienced it yourself. I don't wish that upon anybody. I will always be different now—a little sadder and a little emptier.

Breast-Pumping / Breast-Feeding

Catherine started pumping within twenty-four hours of giving birth. She didn't waste any time. And she was committed. She knew that her breast milk was vital for the health of our twins. She knew every drop was necessary, was absolutely crucial for their nutrition and immune system. Every four hours, like clockwork, she would pump. All day, all night. It bothered her terribly that she couldn't breast-feed. She couldn't nurse our twins because they were too sick and held prisoners in their own tiny incubators. In the beginning they were fed through miniature feeding tubes placed down their noses into their stomachs. They had to eat through those tubes for weeks. Even after several months, they weren't able to eat consistently by breast-feeding. More importantly, we couldn't track their intake by breast-feeding. We couldn't calculate their daily calories unless we were bottle-feeding them. Unfortunately, when you have preemie infants, you find out very quickly that their health and well-being is a numbers game. Constantly weighing, counting, and tracking their intake, counting their calories, always measuring their growth—it became almost an obsession. I hated it. And Catherine hated the fact she couldn't breast-feed on a regular basis. She would occasionally nurse our children, but for the most part, it was nothing but bottle-feeding for our kids.

This carried on for months. She pumped so much at first that we had to store most of her milk in a freezer because when our kids weighed only two to three pounds, they weren't exactly eating like champs. We had a lot of milk left over every day that we would store in the freezer. I know she hated pumping every four hours; it had to have been exhausting. But she did it. She did it because she loved our kids and it was the best thing for them.

It wasn't till the end that her milk supply started to dwindle. The last week she was alive, her output started to decrease. I know that upset her. I obviously had no idea that it bothered her as much as it did. But in hindsight, it clearly pained her that she wasn't able to pump as much milk as she was used to. I remember telling her that it was OK, that she had pumped more milk than anybody could have expected her to. I told her that we had several weeks of her milk stored away in the freezer and that our kids already had the benefit of five months of her pumping. But in the end, my words clearly fell on deaf ears. It didn't matter. I couldn't, and didn't, ease her pain.

After she passed away, I started using the frozen milk we had stored away. Twenty-two days. Five hundred twenty-eight hours was all that it took to use up her entire storage of frozen breast milk. When that ended, I put the twins on formula. I had no choice. They are both doing well and getting bigger. They are slowly climbing the growth chart. They had the benefit of her breast milk for almost six solid months, so their immune systems were able to properly develop. And it shows, because neither of them has gotten sick since they were discharged from the hospital.

I sometimes look back upon that time and wonder how Catherine did it. I wonder how she was able to pump every four hours, spend almost entire days at the hospital with our children, and then take care of them at home after they were discharged while I was at work. I obviously helped out as often as I could, but I still feel guilty at times. And it is this guilt that I am forced to live with.

Cemetery

Over the years Catherine and I made countless decisions together. Thousands. I had known her for half my life, and like any other couple, most of the decisions we made together were insignificant. But like any other couple, some of our decisions carried more weight. Some were more important. These involved where we would live or what kind of house we would end up buying. But the last big decision, our last question to answer, I had to decide, had to answer, by myself. And that was where I was going to lay Catherine to rest. Our last big decision was where I was going to bury my wife.

You never think about where you want to bury your spouse. Why would you? At least at my age, in my thirties, why would you even think about this? It was the furthest thing from my mind. I remember being in a daze driving around the cemetery just seventy-two hours after she passed away. Despite my sadness, despite my tears, I was able to find a spot much more easily than I thought possible. I knew it as soon as I set my eyes on it. I picked a plot on top of a small, gentle hill. It was about thirty yards from the road and located beneath a large tree, yet there was still plenty of sunlight that shone through from the western skyline in the evenings. Catherine always liked trees. In fact, she'd had two separate pictures/prints of trees framed and hung in our house within the past year.

I ended up buying a double plot in the cemetery for when I eventually pass away. I figured I might as well. You never want to contemplate your own mortality, but as I have quickly realized, anything can happen. And when I'm eventually put to rest, I want to be placed next to Catherine, next to my wife, next to my best friend. I also picked out the headstone, a light gray piece of granite with our names inscribed on it. I can't tell you how upsetting it is to see your wife's name carved in a headstone. I also can't explain how surreal it is to see your own name carved next to your wife's, your name with the year you were born neatly placed underneath it followed by a small dash and a blank spot. A blank spot ready to hold the year that will eventually be carved in stone to record your death.

Now I visit the cemetery as often as I can. It's part of my new routine. I can't seem to get there during the week because it's winter and they close the gates at 5:30 p.m. So I try to go every weekend. I'm not even sure why I go, just like I don't even know what I should be doing at times. Unfortunately, there's no manual. There's no instruction booklet. There are no directions to follow when your spouse dies. You just try to figure it out and do the best you can. It's not like I even feel obligated to visit her gravesite. I actually want to go. I still go every week, even though every visit brings a little pain, a little sadness. But for some reason, I feel a little better after I leave. I don't stay long, I never do. I walk up the shallow hill to her gravesite, and it's like slowly turning on a faucet. The tears start to flow by the time I get to the top, and I get incredibly sad. By the time I reach her headstone, it's like I turned on a garden hose.

After I eventually compose myself, I sit down and talk to her. I know this sounds crazy, talking to a gravesite, carrying on a conversation with a headstone. And frankly, before she passed away, I would have readily agreed that it is crazy. But things are different now. I'm different now. I sit down and talk to Catherine. I tell her about the kids. I let her know how well they're doing, how Violet has stopped spitting up like she used to. I tell her how Declan now rolls over and is trying to crawl. I tell her all these things, and I have no idea if she's listening. But I do it anyway. I always finish by telling her that I'm doing the best I can, that I'm taking care of our kids as best I can. And that I love her and always will.

Sometimes after I visit, I walk around the cemetery. I never go far, but I still wander around. I don't know why I do this either. Mostly out of curiosity, I guess. But I always find myself looking at the headstones. Looking at the names and the dates when people died. I especially take notice of couples. I look at when husbands and wives passed away. It's a morbid curiosity, but I can't help it. I've noticed that on almost every headstone, almost every gravesite, the husband died before his wife. Sometimes one year, sometimes twenty years. But it's always the man who passed away first. To be honest, that's the way it's supposed to be. Right or wrong, women are expected to live longer than men. Life-expectancy studies have proven that year after year. This is something I have a hard time accepting. I'd never really thought about it before, but truthfully, I always figured I would die well before Catherine. That's how it's supposed to be. The husband is supposed to die before his wife. For whatever reason, things have been reversed in my life. I have to just make the most of my situation and continue to live.

So I will carry on with my new routine. I plan to continue my visits to the cemetery. But there will eventually come a day when I will visit for the last time. On that day, I'll make that gravesite my permanent home. And after I'm laid to rest, somebody will come along and kneel down by my headstone and start a new inscription. And that person will carve out the year of my death under my name. I just hope, at least for my children's sake, that the year he or she inscribes is several decades in the future.

Cheesin'

Relationships are a growth experience. They have to be or else life and relationships become stagnant, become boring. I grew up and matured over the years with Catherine. I became a responsible adult, and she helped me all along the way. Just as I learned things from her, I taught her various things over the years as well. However, a lot of what I taught her would be considered unimportant or even borderline useless. For some reason, I've always possessed an extraordinary nontraditional, slang vocabulary, words and terms I picked up over the years. Nothing bad, just informal expressions that are not really considered standard. I got a kick out of teaching Catherine different phrases or words. But in the end, on the very last Sunday we spent together before she passed away, she finally taught me a new word, she taught me some slang.

We had gone grocery shopping that weekend. It's actually a little unbelievable when you think about it. We went shopping and bought almost two hundred dollars in groceries, enough food for almost two weeks. We did this four days before she killed herself, which I still can't wrap my head around. Why would you buy groceries and food for two weeks and then end up killing yourself just four days later? But we did, and I thought we had had fun doing it at the time.

She was happy that day, and it showed. On our way out of the store, we passed a stranger who had the largest grin on his face you could ever imagine. He was in his mid- to late twenties and looked like any other guy, except for the fact that he had a comically large smile on his grill, almost cartoonish. As we walked past him, both Catherine and I looked at each other and busted out laughing. We couldn't help it. He just looked so ridiculous. And that's when she taught me a new word, a new phrase that I will forever use and never forget. She said, "Wow, that guy was really cheesin'."

Brilliant. It was absolutely brilliant. I was actually mad at myself for not coming up with that perfectly timed quip. I asked her where she had gotten that word, and she said she'd just made it up. Although I later looked it up in the Urban Dictionary and realized it was an actual, recognized informal expression, although I had never heard that phrase before she had said it. But it fit perfectly. The next several days I would text her while at work and ask her about the kids, because it was about this time when both Declan and Violet were first starting to interact with us. They were actually beginning to smile, and that interaction was amazing. It was like a small miracle every time they would smile at us. I would text Catherine and ask her if any of the kids were "cheesin'" today. That was our little joke. It was our short and abbreviated routine before she died. A few days before she passed, she'd sent me a text message with a picture of Declan sitting in his Nap Nanny with the biggest grin on his face, and the caption was only one word: "Cheesin'!"

I look at that picture to this day, and I still shake my head, mostly out of sadness, out of disbelief. Catherine will never get to see our kids grow up and smile. She will never get to see them enjoy life, which is all she ever wanted for them. I just hope that our kids will never lose their smiles, that they will never stop cheesin'. I want them to grow up to be healthy, to be happy. I also hope that I can one day look in the mirror and smile again myself, at least on occasion. I don't think I will ever smile like that fellow in the grocery store parking lot. But I don't need to, because that was ridiculous. I'm just asking for a little smile, just a little "cheese." That would be enough to make me happy. Is that too much to ask for?

Cleo and Olive

Catherine and I thought about getting a dog. We'd talked about it on and off for years. We even went as far as to research different dog breeds to find the perfect pet. But in the end, we decided—well, I decided—they were too much work, too high maintenance. And in all fairness, I didn't think it would be right to have a dog because we were both working at the time and not able to be at home during the day. Looking back upon this now, it's a little ironic because I now find myself alone, widowed, and taking take of two children, two premature infants who are definitely high maintenance.

In the end, we eventually got two cats, Cleo and Olive, low-maintenance pets, I might add. Catherine loved them. They loved her too. I could tell, and this was especially evident after Catherine was gone. It's weird to think that pets can be affected by the death of their caregivers, but it's absolutely true. Just like humans, cats are creatures of habit. And both of our cats ended up changing their routines after she died.

Cleo and Olive both stayed with me on the longest night of my life, the night after Catherine died, the first night I officially became a widower. After I'd bottle-fed both of my kids, I decided to try to get some sleep, even though I knew it was an act of futility. I didn't even bother closing my eyes that night. I actually didn't want to for fear of what I would see or dream. So I laid on my side of the bed that night, just like I always did, leaving plenty of room for someone who would never need that space again. I faced the bedroom door and just stared blankly ahead, almost numb and completely in shock. I can still remember my cats, both Cleo and Olive, laying down in the bed next to me, and next to each other, for that matter. They also stared at the bedroom door, waiting, with eyes wide open. I remember crying that night, looking at my cats wide awake and waiting. Waiting for Catherine to walk in, to finally get home and come to bed. They didn't know; they couldn't know what had happened. But I could tell they knew something because they didn't sleep at all that night either. It was probably the first time in history that two cats didn't sleep even a minute for an entire night. So all three of us stayed up, staring wide-eyed at the bedroom door. My only movement that night was to wipe away my tears with the back of my hand, only to find my eyes welling up again minutes later.

Fortunately, both of my cats have adjusted. They, of course, eventually went to sleep the following day. In the end, they are cats, animals that generally sleep twenty hours a day. I, on the other hand, was not so lucky. I didn't sleep for the first ninety hours after Catherine passed away. I couldn't. I didn't want to shut my eyes, and the only reason I eventually did was because I succumbed to pure exhaustion, complete fatigue.

Now I find myself taking care of two children and two cats. If not for the help of my in-laws, I wouldn't be able to survive. And for the most part, both my cats seem to be doing relatively well. Except, call me crazy, they both seem a little sad, a little different somehow. Maybe it's just me. Maybe I'm just projecting my pain, my sadness, on them. But I don't think so. We have all had to adjust to a new life without Catherine, the entire family. I don't know exactly how we are going to do this, but we'll find a way, because we have to. We have no choice. Thankfully, there isn't a dog in the mix or I would be woefully outnumbered.

COBRA

The Consolidated Omnibus Budget Reconciliation Act (COBRA) allows workers who lose their health benefits the right to choose to continue their and their family members' health benefits for limited periods of time. This ability to continue your health benefits, or medical insurance, is only available under certain circumstances, such as voluntary or involuntary job loss, reduction in the hours worked, transition between jobs, divorce, or death.

Death. That's where my story comes in. My kids were covered under Catherine's health insurance policy, and, fortunately, she had excellent coverage. After she passed away, I faced a significant dilemma regarding health care for my children. I could certainly switch them to my medical insurance. However, my health insurance plan did not cover their doctors, or even their children's hospital. Both of my kids spent several months in the hospital, and they both had multiple physicians and medical specialty services, all of which were not covered by my insurance.

I'd spent years as a health care provider, basically all my life. Now I could finally see the other side. I could see the side of a health care consumer—and I quickly realized that side is not too pretty.

I decided to sign up for COBRA to provide continuity of care for my children, especially since they required a significant amount of medical supervision. Unfortunately, the transition to COBRA wasn't seamless. In fact, it was a long and painstaking process. In all honesty, it was a nightmare. It ended up taking almost a month to officially obtain COBRA benefits for my children, which, under normal circumstances, wouldn't have been a problem. My kids, however, required multiple prescriptions and needed to go to several doctor's appointments. I ended up spending hours on the phone and faxing countless documents to the insurance company, the last thing I wanted to do after my wife died. I didn't exactly have plans to hang out and go on vacation, but I can promise you I had no desire to spend time on the phone arguing with insurance agents.

In the end, I only had to cancel one doctor's visit because of the delay in coverage from COBRA. It was a cardiology appointment for Declan, a hospital follow-up after his surgery which occurred one month after he was born. After I had checked him in for his appointment, I gave the receptionist his insurance card—an insurance card I had fully expected to be honored. About fifteen minutes later, I was called back to the front desk. I knew I was in trouble. The receptionist told me that there was a problem with Declan's insurance coverage. To put it more bluntly, she said that Declan had no insurance. The sad part was, I was not terribly surprised. I had little to no faith in the system, especially after having dealt with it from the other side for most of my life. I told her to wait a few minutes, and I proceeded—in vain—to make several phone calls. I spent almost twenty minutes talking to insurance agents and COBRA administrators without success. The short of it was that the insurance company required several more documents proving that Catherine had died. They wanted a letter from her previous employer and a certified copy of her death certificate. The problem was, I generally didn't travel around town with those documents in my side pocket next to my car keys and wallet.

I hung up my phone in disgust, realizing this issue was not going to be settled anytime soon, let alone in the next five minutes. I asked the secretary how much Declan's office visit would be if he was "self-pay," the dreaded term for people without insurance. She ruffled a few papers, clicked some keys on her computer keyboard, and actually looked at me with a straight face as she said, "Well, I can't tell you for sure, but it could range from fifty dollars to three thousand dollars."

My jaw dropped. Ridiculous. Absolutely ridiculous. I work in health care. I run a medical practice. My staff answers similar questions almost daily, given the current economic times. And they never give a three-thousand-dollar spread in response to the question "How much will this visit cost?"

I left the office immediately. Declan was fine; he was actually doing well. I knew he was OK because I'm a cardiologist. I know, I know, I'm not a pediatric cardiologist, but he was doing fine, in my opinion. He was eating, he was sleeping, and he needed his diaper changed on a regular basis. As far as I was concerned, I didn't need to pay someone several thousand dollars to tell me he was doing well.

I rescheduled his appointment for two weeks later. I figured I could fax any paperwork or make any phone calls I needed to and solve the problem within a two-week span. In the end, I actually cut it pretty close. It took another twelve days to resolve the issue and officially sign up my kids for COBRA. I took Declan to his cardiologist appointment two weeks later, and, as expected, he was fine. They did an ultrasound of his heart that day; I watched them do it and actually read it in real time while they were doing it. As predicted, he was cleared from a cardiac standpoint, and everything worked out.

I now have a new respect for my own patients' struggles with the health care system. I can now relate to the nonsense, to the paperwork, to the phone calls people need to make sometimes just to obtain medical coverage. COBRA benefits are obviously beneficial, as long as you factor in the price you have to pay to obtain them.

Moving forward, I now know that I have to verify my children's insurance coverage before any appointments, especially if I ever have to change their coverage. I also have a new sense of what my patients go through. And it sucks, it really does. Being a consumer of health care, worrying about insurance coverage, having sick family members—it's terrible. I just hope that as my kids grow older, as they get bigger, they continue to remain healthy and don't require constant and substantial health care. Because I now realize exactly what I have tried not to think about for the past several years: The health care system is broken, and there is no fix in sight. The only advice I have now is a little superficial, and a lot ridiculous. That advice is to not get sick, because that's the only way to avoid the nonsense of what's called our health care system. That's coming from a physician—and that's pretty sad.

Counting Days

I got in the routine of counting days when my kids where in the hospital. It started more out of disbelief than anything else. A few weeks after they were born, I counted up the days and got to eighteen. In the medical field, at least the adult medical field, more than two weeks is considered a long time to be hospitalized. I just couldn't believe they were in the hospital that long. I eventually realized that several weeks, even several months, in the hospital is considered the norm for premature babies. Nevertheless, that fact is none too reassuring, especially when it involves your own kids.

So I started counting their days in the hospital. It was something to do, something to hope for. I wanted them to be discharged before one month passed. Then the next goal was two months, then three months. Well, Violet made it, partially. She was discharged after seventy-six days in the hospital. However, Declan didn't come home until he'd spent ninety-one days in the joint. Although Violet came home early, she never really escaped the hospital. Catherine would bring her back to her former prison every morning while she sat with Declan, and I would eventually meet them all in Declan's hospital room every evening. That was our routine, painful as it was.

When they both finally made it home, I felt partially whole again. I stopped counting because it was truly a milestone that they made it out of the hospital. Better yet, they were both able to come home without any monitors, oxygen, or hospital equipment. Don't get me wrong, it wasn't easy. They both still had to take medication twice a day, and they both cried constantly, but there was a light at the end of the tunnel. There was real hope for the first time in months. The unfortunate part was, Catherine never saw that light. She never saw that hope. She felt guilty about what had happened. She blamed herself for the kids being born prematurely. She never talked about it, but I know. She also constantly worried about them. She was convinced they were not going to be OK, that they'd get sick again or they wouldn't grow up normally, which may happen, by the way. But I can't think like that. Not now, not ever. Especially after what I've been through. I hope for the best and whatever happens, happens. I can't let myself be negative, not when it comes to my kids.

I was finally done counting days—until September 27, 2012, the day Catherine killed herself. One hundred forty days after she gave birth. Sixty-four days after Violet was discharged from the hospital. Forty-nine days after Declan was allowed to escape. Since then, I've started counting days again. I obviously know that counting the days since my wife died serves absolutely no purpose. I realize this, but I can't stop. I consider myself a fairly practical guy, someone who doesn't engage in useless activities. I acknowledge that this is an exercise in futility, an exercise with no end in sight. I completely understand that I can count forever, because she's not coming back. I can count days until I die, and there really is no point. But I continue to count, just the same.

Every morning when I come to work, the first person I see is my office manager, who, by the way, has been great through all this. I think she treats me like a son, which is OK by me. It's always nice to have people care about you. I've grown to appreciate this fact as time goes on.

Every morning when she asks me how I'm doing, I respond with a lie. I tell her, "I'm fine" or "I'm OK," which clearly is not the case. Sometimes I mention the days, the number of days since Catherine passed away. The past several weeks, she's told me to stop, which I understand is the obvious thing to do. But I can't.

And today, the day I'm typing these words on my keyboard, it's been seventy-six days since my wife killed herself. My office manager told me to start counting other things, which, I think, is actually a great idea. However, I can't seem to come up with an acceptable alternative. It's not for lack of ideas.

Let's see. I can count the number of times I've visited my wife's gravesite this week (three). Or I can count the number of Kleenex boxes I've used up while commuting to work this past month (two). Or I can count the number of times I lied to people this past week when they asked me how I was doing and I responded, "OK" (eight). Or I can count the number of hours I was awake last night staring at the ceiling because I couldn't sleep (five). Or I can the count the number of years that will pass until my kids start asking me what happened to their mother (?).

Well, none of the above really works for me. At least, not yet. So I will continue to count the days, right or wrong. I do hope I will reach a point in my life when I can stop. I'm not sure that day will ever come. I just really don't know. Maybe that day will finally arrive. But until then, the counting will continue.

Curtains

Over the course of my life, Catherine imprinted herself on me, on my very existence. It's an expected consequence, especially when you've known someone as long as I knew Catherine. We met during our freshman year in undergrad, when we were both eighteen years old, and she died forty-three days short of my thirty-sixth birthday, not to mention forty-seven days shy of our eighth wedding anniversary. So I knew her over half my life, which sounds about right, because I now feel exactly half empty, and that accurately describes how I feel these days. I'm no longer a whole person.

I still function. I still go to work. I still come home at the end of the day. And I still take care of my kids, which is probably the only thing that gets me through the days now. But I'm not the same. The half of me that feels empty is now consumed with sadness, which is something I have accepted. But I try to hold onto the things that Catherine brought into my life. Memories, mostly. I try to focus on the good times, the life we had before everything changed. Before she was put on bed rest and our lives were turned upside down. But I also turn to the tangible things in my life, which include everything I look at when I come home.

Ever since the day we bought our house, Catherine spent time shaping and molding it into our dream home. She'd just about accomplished that goal by the time she got pregnant. She had impeccable taste, incredible style—that is indisputable. She knew what looked good and used her taste to decorate our entire house. She picked out furniture, rugs, lamps, kitchen appliances, everything. It all made sense, and at the same time, it was all her, very distinctive, very tasteful. She would often humor me and ask my opinion on something. But let's be honest, I'm a typical guy. As long as it didn't look too feminine, nothing pink, I was in full agreement because what the hell did I know? I'm fairly honest with my shortcomings, which are many. I have no idea when it comes to interior decorating. So I was glad Catherine took charge and slowly transformed our house into her vision. Again, it all made sense, and it looked great.

But now I'm alone, by myself, in our house that my wife spent over two years building, shaping, and decorating. For some people, I can understand it could be too much. But I need it. I need the constant reminder. I walk around my house and remember Catherine. I remember how she agonized about the purchase of one particular rug. Or how she couldn't decide between two different dining room tables but eventually picked the perfect one, which she always did. I see all the things she did, and I smile, which is a rare thing these days. Because I know I was by her side every step of the way while she put together our house.

The best thing was, if she couldn't find the exact thing she was looking for, she would just do it herself. She spent days trying to find the perfect curtains for the upstairs windows. Hours on the Internet, searching, Googling, but nothing. She couldn't find the exact pattern, the perfect look that she had in mind. So she just decided to make the curtains herself. That's another of the countless things I loved about her. She was so talented. She had so much to offer. If she didn't like something, she wouldn't settle for the next best option. She would take charge and do what she could to find a solution. And if it took actually crafting or creating what she wanted, well, that's just what she did. She couldn't find the perfect curtains, so she picked out a fabric pattern and made her own curtains. She wasn't a seamstress; this wasn't a hobby for her. But it didn't matter. She taught herself how to sew, picked out a pattern, and made it happen.

Now when I go upstairs and see her curtains, I smile. I know the hard work she put into making those curtains to complete her vision, and I smile. That's one of the reasons why I don't want to move. I like my house. No, I love my house. And I love what Catherine did with it. I hold onto the memories of her shaping our dream home. And for a brief moment, if only for a second, I let myself smile.

Customer Service

Good customer service is hard to come by. I don't even expect it anymore; I haven't for years. But I do expect adequate customer service, just enough baseline knowledge to help solve my problem, and a little common sense. This last part, common sense, is the problem. At least it was for the two to three weeks after Catherine died.

I must have talked to fifteen different customer service representatives after she passed away. You don't realize what you have to do when a loved one dies until the situation presents itself. You have to cancel credit cards, close out bank accounts, change utility bills, contact 401(k) retirement services, and deal with the government for social security benefits for the kids, just to name a few.

The problem—well, one of the problems—was that almost ninety-five percent of the people I talked to followed the same script and wouldn't deviate from it. I would start every phone conversation explaining that my wife had died and that I needed to cancel this account or close that account and so on. At first, everybody was very sorry and tried to sound sympathetic, which is somewhat nice and completely expected. However, by the end of almost every conversation, the customer service representative would always finish the phone call with "And have a great day!"

Again, I realize that they are just doing their jobs and following a script. But I can't tell you how many times I just wanted to reply, "Well, having a great day is probably not on my to-do list because, you know, my wife just killed herself."

But I never said that, no matter how upset I got. I always just shook my head and hung up the phone. Thankfully, I don't have to deal with all those phone calls anymore. I have taken care of all the "logistics." Sadly, I still haven't checked "Have a great day" off my to-do list yet. I hope that will change one day. It would be nice to get up in the morning and look forward to a great day again. It definitely would be something special to go to bed at night and feel like everything will be OK. Hopefully, with the help of my children, I can accomplish that goal.

Dating

Not an option. I'm not ready—so let's move on.

Derailed

I reflect upon my life and wonder. I wonder what I've done and how I landed in this situation. I just can't understand how I arrived at my current destination. This may sound sort of strange, for a "young" guy in his thirties to reflect, to look back upon his life, but that's what I do sometimes.

Growing up, I never had a vision or master plan for my life. I never had a set schedule or an instruction book to follow. I was just like you or anybody else; I grew up and wanted the American Dream. I wanted to be happy, part of a family, and successful in life, whatever that means. I only bring this up because of what my therapist asked me the other day. And trust me, I really can't believe I've become one of those people who start sentences with what their therapist says. But that's what happens. That's what becomes of you when your wife kills herself and you're left alone with two newborn children.

My therapist asked me the other day about my life. He thought it was instructive to ask me about my "life plan." He actually said, "So, everything was going well until Catherine was put on bed rest. So, things were going pretty well until then, right?"

I couldn't believe the question. It was ridiculous, to say the least. I readily admit I'm not a psychiatrist or do I play one on TV, but this was downright absurd. Nobody plans on this sort of tragedy, this sort of life plan. Like I said, I wanted what everybody else wants in life. Happiness. Nobody plans on this sort of tragedy, this sequence of events. Nobody expects his wife to go on bed rest five months into her pregnancy. Nobody plans on his wife being hospitalized, giving birth to twins three months early, and having their kids hospitalized for another three months. Another three months of darkness. And to top it off, nobody expects his wife to commit suicide, to kill herself to end her pain yet giving birth to someone's else pain—mine.

So that's how my life became unglued. That's when I was derailed. And to my therapist's point, I never planned on this. I never expected this, but who does? Who really does? Yes, my life was pretty good before this happened. And yes, things were coming along as planned, if there really was, in fact, a life plan. But one could never expect this, this sort of sadness, this sort of tragedy.

I'm doing the best I can. At least I think so. People say it will get better. Personally speaking, I doubt it. Maybe the pain will start to dull a little over time and the emptiness will not be so vast. Maybe it won't. But it will always be there, and I have accepted that. I can only hope that my life will get back on the tracks again and that I won't be derailed forever. That I can one day recover. So I'm doing the best I can. The best I can for my kids, and that's the only thing I can hope for.

Desperados Under the Eaves

Don't the sun look angry through the trees
Don't the trees look like crucified thieves
Don't you feel like desperados under the eaves
Heaven help the one who leaves
(Warren Zevon)

Discharge Day

It all sort of hit home that day. Reality set in, and it wasn't pretty, especially for Catherine. She was discharged from the hospital three days after she gave birth to our kids. Mind you, she was hospitalized on bed rest for nine days prior to going into labor, so she hadn't been home in almost two weeks. After we packed up all our things, all our belongings from her hospital room, we stopped by the neonatal intensive care unit (NICU) to see our kids. They were both still in incubators at that time and would be for the foreseeable future. They were also hooked up to a breathing apparatus, a continuous positive airway pressure (CPAP) machine, because they were unable to breathe on their own. They were still very sick, but stable for the time being. It was early afternoon, and the plan was to take our stuff home and then come right back to the hospital to see our kids.

We took the elevator down to the hospital lobby with all our belongings, and Catherine waited by the exit while I got the car. When I pulled it around, we methodically loaded it up with all of our meaningless items—pillows, clothes, flowers, books—in silence. After we got in and shut the car doors, Catherine lost it. She doubled over in tears, just uncontrollable sorrow and despair. Because it wasn't supposed to be like this. This was not how she'd envisioned her pregnancy, her birthing experience, her children, her life. You're supposed to take your kids home from the hospital on your discharge day. Your kids shouldn't be lying upstairs in the NICU, sick, weak, and helpless, not able to breathe for themselves. Getting discharged and going home is supposed to be one of the happiest moments for a family. Taking your baby home, starting your new life, raising your healthy children in your own house—that's what was missing, and Catherine wept. All I could do was hold her, comfort her. And that's what I did. But it never felt right. Because it never was right, going home just to put things away and then come right back. But that's what we did. Day after day after day, we went to the hospital to see our kids. Although her tears dried up at times, they always came back because of how sick our kids were. It pained me because I couldn't do anything about it. I was helpless, even though I was their father. I was helpless. And Catherine felt that way too.

Doctor's Appointments

I hate them. I absolutely can't stand doctor's appointments, which is funny because I'm a physician. If my patients didn't keep their doctor's appointments, I'd be out of work. But it's a whole new ball game when it comes to my children. Without stating the obvious, it's different when you have to take your own kids to the doctor. But really, what parent enjoys taking kids to the doctor? For Catherine and me, it was particularly grueling, especially because we had to take the twins to so many appointments. Kidney doctors, eye doctors, heart doctors, preemie doctors, plain ol' regular baby doctors—you pick a specialist, and we would have to take our kids to an appointment. Their appointments came fast and furiously, at least in the beginning. That's how it was after they were first discharged from the hospital. It was part of our new routine. One, two, sometimes three days a week Catherine would have to pack up the babies and take them to the doctors. I would try to make as many of their appointments as I could but I usually missed most of them because I had to be at work. Back then, Catherine was scared to take the twins to the doctors. She would never admit it, but I know she was. She was fearful the doctors would tell her bad news or that our kids hadn't gained enough weight. She hated seeing the growth charts and having it pointed out that both of our kids were well below the 10 percent line. She felt helpless and, unfortunately, blamed herself.

Now that she's gone, I've taken over the routine. I've had to adjust my work schedule, but I really don't have a choice. It was never really even an option because the buck stops with me. I'm the only one left to take care of them. It's been a rude awakening to being a single father, to being widowed. Fortunately, the twins' appointment schedule has slowed down. I don't find myself taking them every week, or even every other week like it was a few months ago, which means my kids are doing better, they are slowly getting healthier, getting stronger. At this point, that's all I'm trying to focus on, because anytime I let my mind wander, anytime I'm not completely focused on my kids, I start to think of Catherine. And that's when the sadness seeps in. That's when the pain takes root. That's when I feel like giving up, even though I know that's not a choice. Because I have my kids to care of. They need me as much as I need them. I plan on taking them to as many doctor's appointments as they need in the future. As long as they are "well visit" appointments, I'll be happy. Well, as happy as I can hope to be.

Elephant in the Room

I have always liked elephants. I'm not sure why, but they seem like nice, intelligent animals. Although they seem larger than life, they always appear very peaceful, harmless, despite their massive bodies. It's unfortunate that I only see them in zoos, caged up. But that's how I feel sometimes. At least, that's what it was like when I first returned back to my job after my wife died. I felt like the elephant in the room.

The first week back at work was the worst by far. I remember walking around the hospital trying to keep my head down, trying desperately not to make eye contact with anybody. No matter how hard I tried, I felt like everybody was watching me, staring at me. It was worse when I did finally look people in the eyes, because all I could see was pity, was sorrow. And I saw it from everybody—from nurses, techs, other doctors, and mostly from my patients. It was worse when people would look at me but not say anything. I'd rather they asked me questions or voiced their concern. I'd rather they said something, anything, which would be better than their silently acknowledging my tragedy but verbally ignoring it. Although going back to work was tough, and interacting with people was tougher, I never blamed people for their responses, for how they interacted with me. In fact, everybody was very supportive and seemed to honestly care and sympathize.

But it didn't make it any easier. The hospital staff's support and my patients' caring thoughts were absolutely appreciated, but in the end nothing could actually take my pain away. As time passed, as the days rolled on, things did eventually get better, a little easier. Although my sadness has never lessened, has not softened, I'm no longer treated as a hard-luck case. I'm no longer the elephant in the room, because people always move on, they always revert back to their normal routine. Don't get me wrong, people still do occasionally ask me questions, inquire about my children, and always wish me well. But for the most part, it's business as usual back at work. And trust me, that is fine by me. Although I think I can never really live a normal existence from here on out, the closer to that goal I can achieve, the better off I will be. Although being a giant, larger-than-life animal with a really cool trunk seems great, nobody ever wants to be the elephant in the room.

Errands

Nobody really enjoys doing errands. In all honesty, who likes to spend the weekend or time off shopping for stuff you don't really want but will eventually use? How fun is it to go the store to buy paper towels, detergent, soap, or toothpaste? But it never really seemed like an errand for us, for Catherine and me. Don't get me wrong, I never looked forward to buying toilet paper on a Saturday afternoon; however, it was something we always did together, running errands. We would go to the store about twice a month and do our shopping. We would walk around, talk, share, and, most importantly, poke fun at stuff we saw. I miss that now. It's not something I was ever really aware of before, because it was just natural, just another thing we did together, like everything else in life. It's almost comparable to the air we breathe. You don't really notice it because we breathe in and out all day long without thinking about it. However, if I took away your oxygen, it would definitely get your attention. It's sort of like that. Having Catherine in my life, having her by my side every day to talk to, to plan with, to run errands with, to live life together, just seemed natural. It wasn't magic, which is what Tom Hanks said in *Sleepless in Seattle*, because I don't believe in that nonsense. We just fit together, and now that she's gone, it's hard to move on. I still get up every day. I still go to the store and buy mindless items that I think I need and do eventually use. But it's still difficult because I am always alone when I run my errands. I feel like I am missing a part of me everywhere I go, no matter what I'm doing. Sometimes I walk around in sort of a daze because I struggle to breathe, almost like I am out of oxygen. That's how I feel now that she's gone. All I can do is struggle to breathe.

Fire and Rain

I've seen fire and I've seen rain
I've seen sunny days that I thought would never end
I've seen lonely times when I could not find a friend
But I always thought that I'd see you again
(James Taylor)

Funeral

It's interesting that you try to look your best for a day you know you'll feel your worst. I know that it's customary and it's tradition, and for the most part, it's out of respect for the deceased, but it's still rather odd when you think about it. But that's what I did. I had my black suit dry-cleaned because I hadn't worn it in almost two years. I even got a haircut the day before one of the longest and strangest days of my life, my wife's funeral.

I don't really recall all the details from the day I buried my wife. I think that's a good thing because it was a very surreal, painful day. I remember moments of pure despair and sadness. I remember almost falling down because I was too consumed with emotion. I also recall shaking hands, receiving hugs, and hearing people's kind words and condolences, although I couldn't tell you what people said to me on that day, not exactly. I knew most of the people who came, but a lot of them were complete strangers, either friends or family of my in-laws or people who had worked with Catherine whom she may or may not have mentioned, people I'd never met. But I do remember all the people were nice, they were all respectful, and they were all genuinely sad, which is not surprising, because Catherine was an amazing person. One of a kind. Whoever came in contact with her knew it.

At the end of the day, at the cemetery, I remember standing by her closed coffin, one hand on the cold, wooden lid. I just stood there, by myself, although I really wasn't alone. There were still some people left from the funeral in the background, watching me. I felt such sadness at that moment, such emptiness. I felt alone, and I didn't know what I should do. Nobody prepares you for this, as nobody should, because nobody should bury their spouse, even though that's impossible and can never be predicted. But that's how I feel. It's one of the worst things you could ever do in life, bury your wife. That's why I will probably never remarry, mostly because I could never meet another person as special or as wonderful as Catherine. But a part of me never wants to go through this again. Since there are no guarantees in life, I don't think I could handle another tragedy like this ever again. It's just too much to take on, too much sadness, too much pain. Once was enough, and that was enough for me.

Graduate School

Life is all about timing, isn't it? Good luck. Bad luck. Success. Failure. A lot of which you can control, but some things you can't. When Catherine and I first started to date, timing wasn't on our side. Just a few months into the relationship, she ended up moving four hours away to start her master's degree in graduate school while I stayed at home and started medical school. I had known Catherine for several years by that point, but we really had only started going out recently.

But we made it work, just like we always did. And it wasn't a problem. I admit it was a little inconvenient, and I would have much rather lived in the same city at that time, but the long distance between us didn't slow us down. We took turns. Every other weekend one of us would make a four-hour trip, each way, to see each other. This carried on for two years. I think at the time it made our relationship stronger. We talked in the evenings during the week. This was well before cell phones and text messages, long before FaceTime and Skype. Back then I bought twenty-dollar phone cards at the local gas station and used those minutes to talk on the phone. This was back in 1999, a lifetime ago, when things were different, when we were younger.

After two years she finished up her master's degree and moved back home. By that point, I knew she was the one. There was no question. I knew we would eventually get married and that it was only a matter of time. After Catherine worked for a few years, she made the decision to go back to school. This time she went to law school, and this time around she stayed in the same city. We got married in her first year of law school, and at that time I thought we'd be married forever. Well, at least longer than seven years. But we didn't quite make it; she died just six weeks shy of our eighth wedding anniversary. For whatever reason, it wasn't meant to be, and that's what I struggle with now. After all the years I'd known Catherine, after all the time spent together, after all the ups, all the downs, and after all the love we'd shared together, she's gone. Sometimes I think if I'd done something differently, I would have been able to prevent this from happening, this tragedy. But I can't change the past, and now all I have to look to is the future, the future with my children.

Growing Old Alone

This is not something I initially thought of. But as the days go by, the shock slowly wanes, and reality sets in, it's something I think about often now. I know I have plenty of things to occupy my time over the coming years, first and foremost my kids, then my career. But I also think about what it's going to be like to grow old alone, to retire by myself.

People tell me that I'm a young guy, that "You'll never know what will happen." I know they're implying that maybe one day I'll meet somebody else. But the problem is, I don't want to meet anybody else. I know I can't replace Catherine. I can't replace my wife or my children's mother. That's the problem. I can't. And I've accepted that. But along with acceptance comes sadness and reality.

Sometimes I get reminded of this, and I think about my life and what has happened. I met a guy at a restaurant last week. It was a rare night out for me when a friend took me out for dinner. It was nice to get away. But I can never truly escape, and that's the problem. This guy sitting next to us at the bar started talking about his life, his problems. He was obviously a few drinks in, more like several stiff drinks into the evening, but I'll never forget him or what he said. He was about sixty-five years old, and he said that his wife had died of cancer thirty-five years ago. He sort of talked tough about it, like it didn't bother him, but I could tell it did. He talked about never having kids, about never remarrying, about his life now. And I grew sad—for him and for myself.

I could see the pain in his eyes. You might not have seen it. You would just see another poor man drinking away his sorrows at the bar. But I saw past that. I knew that look. I understood that look he had in his eyes. I see the same thing every morning when I get up and look in the mirror. I see the same thing every evening when I turn in for another sleepless night. I have the same look in my own eyes as that poor guy I met at the bar—emptiness.

Grunts of Insanity

Nobody can prepare you for parenting a premature baby, let alone premature twins. It's impossible. There is too much to know, and yet there are too many unknowns. One thing they certainly didn't tell us about was the grunts, what Catherine and I so fondly named the "grunts of insanity."

We didn't hear the grunts for the first six weeks after our kids were born because they were sheltered, kept away from the elements and held up in tiny plastic incubators for their protection. We had no idea the babies constantly grunted while they were awake. But we found out soon enough when Violet finally escaped her little plastic prison. I remember the day she was strong enough to be placed in a regular crib in the NICU. That's when it started; well, at least that's when we first heard the grunts. Almost all day, she would constantly grunt. It was unrelenting and pervasive, constant and unforgiving, something you would hear filtering out of an insane asylum.

At first, Catherine and I were terrified. We had no idea what was going on. But the physicians, the nurses, the entire NICU staff reassured us that this was completely normal for premature babies. For some reason, since they are so young and their nervous systems are not quite developed yet, premature babies are known for grunting. Of course, Catherine was not happy with that explanation. So she did as she always did; she turned to the Internet for more information and did some research. She searched for another possible explanation for the grunts of insanity. She quickly discovered exactly what everybody else had told us, that this just happens and infants eventually outgrow this phase. Although this seemed like a reasonable and acceptable consequence of their prematurity, Catherine absolutely hated it. She hated the nonstop grunting and envisioned our children being twelve years old, walking around the house not talking, just grunting constantly.

It continued, for both Declan and Violet, even after we took them home from the hospital. It would go on and on, at times all through the night, relentlessly. Sometimes it would sound like a demented symphony if they were both awake at the same time. Thankfully, Violet eventually stopped about two weeks after we brought her home from the hospital. But Declan continued on, like a grunting champ. His grunts did eventually become less frequent, less vocal, but they were still present when Catherine passed away. He was still grunting along at that time. But he too eventually stopped. It took another two weeks or so, and by October I was finally living in a grunt-free household. Unfortunately, Catherine was no longer alive to witness this. She wasn't here with me to experience the blissful silence. That hurt, because although the grunts of insanity have since passed, they have been replaced with the pained silence of emptiness, the emptiness I now have in my heart. I just hope that one day the emptiness will be filled with the joy and laughter of two happy, healthy children. Either way, I call it a small victory now that the grunts have finally faded away.

Guilt

I start walking downstairs, but everything appears different. Yet something is all too familiar at the same time. It's getting dark outside, and it looks like the sun is setting. All the lights are off, every single one in the house. I find my way downstairs and it hits me. I'm back home. I'm actually at the house I grew up in as a child. I look in the family room, and my dad's asleep on the couch. Well, he looks asleep. I start walking toward him, and the doorbell rings, but it's not the same doorbell I remember. There is a long, ear-piercing chime that goes on for what seems like an eternity. My dad doesn't move. He sort of looks like he's asleep, but for some reason I don't think he's really asleep. I turn to open the door and I find my old childhood friend, dressed in the same clothes I remember from the 1980s. Yet he's older. He's my age. I haven't spoken to him in decades, for good reason. He was a nice enough kid, from what I remember, but I stopped hanging out with him because he was always looking for trouble, or causing it. He doesn't even say hello and runs past me. He seems upset, or at least nervous. He doesn't say a word either; he just stands there in the hallway and looks at me. Well, more like stares at me. It's unclear what he wants. As the chimes finally drift away, I start to ask a question but am cut off.

I hear sirens—loud, charging sirens—screaming up the road toward my house. It sounds like somebody sent a whole fleet of cop cars, maybe even an army. I should be confused, but I'm not. I should be nervous or scared, but I'm not. I turn and look at my dad on the couch, but now his eyes are open. He's just looking at me, still not saying a word. He doesn't need to; I can tell he's upset. I can sense he's angry with me. Well, more like disappointed. I just stand—in complete darkness at this point because the sun has set—and listen to the sirens as they draw closer and closer. Then the phone rings. I don't remember having a phone in this room when I was a child, but there it is, on a table in the corner. Before I can move, my friend picks up the phone, never taking his eyes off me, as if he's scared I will leave, as if I will turn and run. As he holds the phone close to his ear, he remains absolutely silent, never saying a word. He just nods his head several times and continues to stare at me. As he hangs up the phone, I open my mouth to say something, anything, and my dad cuts me off. Still motionless, with eyes of disappointment, he speaks from the couch. He says in a dead, hollow tone, "They're coming for you, son. They're coming for you."

Before I can comprehend his sentence, before I can question his words, my friend finally decides to speak. "The police are here. They're coming to pick you up. They're here to arrest you." Before he finishes, I understand. I finally realize what this is all about. I look at both my dad and my friend with sad eyes full of tears, and my friend says in a quiet monotone voice, "They're coming to arrest you for the death of your wife. The police are here to book you for Catherine's murder."

Then I wake up. Then the dream—well, the nightmare—is over. This was a recurrent theme after Catherine passed away. It was amazing I even slept an hour, let alone a solitary minute, after she died. That was when I knew I was in trouble, I knew I needed help. About three weeks after my wife died, I finally did something I never thought I'd do. I'd finally encountered something I couldn't handle on my own. I picked up the phone and scheduled an appointment. I made an appointment with a therapist.

Hard Habit to Break
Now being without you
Takes a lot of getting used to
Should learn to live with it
But I don't want to

Being without you
Is all a big mistake
Instead of getting easier
It's the hardest thing to take
I'm addicted to you, babe
You're a hard habit to break
(Chicago)

H_2O

It's funny how certain things can trigger a memory, or more specifically, trigger pain. I was having a usual day—well, as ordinary a day as I can expect—and all of a sudden it hit me. I had woken up particularly early that morning. I had to be up and out of the house by 5:00 a.m. in order to round on patients before coming to the office. Needless to say, I was physically and mentally drained, and it was only 9:00 a.m. I was also way past my usual coffee limit; I was sucking down my fourth cup of joe between office patients when I headed to the restroom for a much needed break. As I returned to the office, all I could think about was rehydrating and getting some water. However, the sad part about my office is there is no way to get acceptable drinking water. The so-called "water" out of the faucet at work is undrinkable, and I don't even consider myself a water snob. For some reason, we don't have a water dispenser, nor do we have any water bottles in the mini break room/kitchen. That's when it hit me. That's when I stopped dead in my tracks.

I'd had this very same complaint about a year ago, and I'd told Catherine about it. Not even a week later, she'd bought me a mini personal desktop water purifier and dispenser. That's what she did for me, what she always did for me. Those little things that you can't really relate to people when they try to comfort you and say, "Everything will be OK." Well, actually, no, everything won't be OK because there is nobody in my life who can truly understand me like Catherine did.

I took the much-needed water dispenser to work, and while it was quite functional, it was a little slow. Still, I used it every day when I was in the office. At least I did until our lives changed, until we were derailed.

When Catherine was placed on bed rest, the only real medical advice offered was that she should stay hydrated and drink plenty of fluids. Now, when your doctor or a medical professional recommends that you increase your water intake, you might expect that you would drink maybe three or four glasses of water a day. That's not exactly what Catherine did. She would literally drink water all damn day. From morning until night, she drank water. It was actually worse after she was hospitalized. I can remember in excruciating detail how many times I refilled her water bottles. She always drank that damn water. She would complain about it at times, and toward the end, right before she went into premature labor, she actually grew to disdain water. But it still didn't stop her. She was always there, lying in bed or sitting in a chair, drinking water.

I eventually took her gift, the water dispenser that she had gotten me, from the office and brought it home to place in our bedroom. The only problem was that the dispenser happened to be extraordinarily loud, something I hadn't noticed before because I always had music playing in the background when I did my notes at work. When I took it home and plugged it into the bedroom, it was actually quite loud and not really conducive to sleep. That little experiment lasted about forty-eight hours. But for some reason, I never brought it back to the office.

That particular day—when I had awakened early, struggled through the first several hours of the day drinking cup after cup of coffee, then finally wished for some H_2O—I remembered Catherine. I remembered everything just like it was yesterday. I remembered Catherine drinking glass after glass of water at home, then drinking bottle after bottle of water at the hospital after she was admitted for inpatient bed rest. That's when I broke down at work, thinking about my wife and what she went through.

It's funny like that. You go about your day and all of a sudden a memory gets triggered and you're taken back to the past, to the past when your wife was alive. You remember certain things in excruciating detail. That's when the pain sets in. The emptiness follows. That's when it's everything I can do to not just give up, because I have two children who depend on me. And that's what matters now. So now I try to bring bottled water with me to work because I have to stay hydrated. When I don't, I remember. I remember what it was like for Catherine, and I hurt.

Halloween

Every day is basically the same. Sad. Even now, and it's been several months. My life, my new routine—pretty much the same. Every day, with few exceptions, I get up and miss my wife. I go to work and miss my wife. I drive home and miss my wife. Brief moments of happiness eventually do shine through when I hold and feed my kids, despite the onslaught of crying and fussiness. Then I try to go to sleep, but instead I end up lying wide awake in bed and miss my wife. Set, repeat, and move forward.

Eventually, as time goes by and days roll on to the next, certain events, certain holidays arrive and break up the monotony, break up my routine. Unfortunately, these days don't offer any sort of reprieve. Instead, they provide a new level of emptiness I struggle to deal with. That's what happened as the end of October rolled around. Halloween marked the beginning of an emotional boot camp I was in no shape to participate in, but time has no friends. As the days passed, I was forced to engage in my own personal feast of despair, a monumental dinner of sadness.

At the time, my prospects, my immediate future, weren't too appetizing. Looking past Halloween, the menu didn't appear too forgiving. The meal started with an appetizer, my thirty-sixth birthday, in early November. The soup-and-salad course followed with what would have been our wedding anniversary in mid-November. Then came the main course, the heart of the meal, which, of course, was Thanksgiving. And you can't forget dessert, a nice, classic dessert—Christmas. To finish, you need an after-dinner drink, which was New Year's Eve, a great way to toast the end of any terrific meal.

So that's what was in store for me, a feast for the ages, a definite break from my routine. Unfortunately, believe it or not, I wasn't in the mood, not in the slightest. But what could I do? Like I said, time has no friends. As the days marched on, I had no choice but to dig in, make the best of my life, and deal with my sadness.

Halloween was never a classic day for Catherine and me. We would occasionally go to a Halloween party. We would sometimes even dress up, but it was never considered a big event. Until now, until we had kids. A few weeks before she passed away, Catherine talked about possible costumes for our kids. She mostly joked about it, but there was some seriousness to her suggestions, to her thoughts. She had envisioned a lion costume for Violet. Don't ask me why, or even how, but that's what she joked about. So as the day approached, Catherine's sister, Sandy, took it upon herself to actually hand-make a lion costume for my daughter. To be honest, I had my doubts. But in the end, she did a hell of a job with that costume. It fit Violet perfectly. And for Declan, Sandy found a funny baby "business executive" costume, complete with a tie and dress shirt.

That night, after I put some candy in a bowl on the front porch, we dressed up my kids in their costumes. At that age, they didn't last too long, just enough time to snag some photos. Then the crying began. Holding them in their silly costumes brought my own tears. All I could think of was how much I wanted Catherine to be here, to share this moment with us. I wanted to talk to her, to joke with her, to take pictures and laugh. Because that's what we used to do together, laugh. No matter how things were going, we could always make each other laugh, even if it was just for a moment, or even just for a second. I miss that, among a million other things. I know I will never get that back again.

That was my Halloween; that was my appetizer. As I looked ahead at the rest of the menu, I decided to loosen my belt and buy some more

Kleenex, because it was looking like I had one hell of a meal in front of me.

Hurricane Sandy and the Blackout

Bad luck. That's the only thing I can come up with. There's no other explanation. Trust me, I realize that Hurricane Sandy caused a lot more pain and suffering for millions of other people compared to me, especially people on the East Coast, and I sympathize. I know it inflicted life-altering tragedy and death on families. But I had already experienced my own tragedy, my own death, approximately one month before the storm hit. Even though I live in the Midwest, even though I was hundreds of miles from the East Coast, Hurricane Sandy still inflicted damage, still caused some more pain for my already beaten-down soul.

I should have gotten out of the house sooner. I should have left the house as soon as I got home from work. That's what I remember when I look back upon that storm. But for some reason, I thought I wouldn't lose power. I thought everything would be all right. Again, I have no rational explanation for this belief. In retrospect, I should have expected the worst, but at the time, I didn't. We lost power at about eight o'clock the evening the storm hit. When the lights went out, I knew we had to leave. Thankfully, my mother-in-law was there to help me gather up the kids and their belongings. As the wind howled and the rain beat down, we took the kids to my in-laws' house.

That was another long night. Although my in-laws never lost power, the gusting wind and the rain were ridiculously loud and almost unbearable. I didn't sleep that night, which wasn't unusual for me back then (and even now). I remember lying in bed, eyes wide open, thinking about all the terrible things that could be happening to my house, the house I had to abandon because we lost power. I envisioned shingles ripping off and trees falling down on my roof, breaking windows and causing significant water damage. I ended up getting out of bed at 4:00 a.m. I hadn't slept, so the time of day didn't really matter to me. I quickly checked on the kids and then I headed back to my house. I remember pulling into my driveway, reassured because I didn't see a large tree collapsed on my roof. I took my flashlight out of my trunk and did a quick survey of the house in the dark. I checked every room from ceiling to floor, hoping for the best but expecting the worst. After I made a quick pass, I felt relief wash over me as everything seemed OK. But for some reason, I wasn't completely satisfied. That's when I made a second pass. And that's when I found the water damage.

It all seemed rather appropriate, in a sick and twisted way, another sad chapter in my tale of woes. I went back into the babies' room and soon discovered the problem. When I shone the flashlight on the ceiling, my heart sank. There was significant water damage in the corner of the room, water slowly trickling down the wall and onto my son's crib. All I could do was shake my head in disbelief. This was not something I needed right now. This was not something I felt ready to handle after everything I'd already been through. I was just one month out from burying my wife, and the last thing I needed was to lose power from a hurricane that struck hundreds of miles away and find water dripping on my son's crib.

So I gathered myself and did what I've always done—my best. I cleaned up what I could in the dark with my small flashlight. I threw a bunch of towels on the ground in hopes that the hardwood floors would not also be damaged, and I drove to work. It was still five in the morning, much too early to call any contractors, to call any roofers. Later that day, that's exactly what I did. I also called my homeowner's insurance company and filed a claim. For the next six days, I lived at my in-laws' house because that's how long it took to restore my power. I checked on my house every morning before work and every evening after work for those six days. For some reason, I thought my bad luck would continue. I thought that something else would happen, something terrible.

I kept thinking my house would be broken into because it was obvious I had no power, no electricity. Thankfully, this never happened. And again, I know that the people on the East Coast lost power and sustained far greater damage than I did. But six days with no power when the storm struck five hundred miles away—I couldn't believe it. I later found out that the local electric companies had farmed out their electricians, sending them east to help the communities and people on the coast. That was a wonderful idea, except it left the local people, the people in my city, without power and without contractors to fix the blackouts here.

I eventually got my electricity restored. I also had contractors repair my roof and fix the water damage in my children's room. I eventually got everything back to the way it was, at least back to how it was before the storm hit. It will never be back to how it was one month earlier, when I still had a wife and my kids still had a mother. But I can't think like that anymore. I know I have to look ahead, because every time I look back all I see is pain, all I see is blackness. I had enough of the blackness after Hurricane Sandy caused me to lose power. At this point, I just want to see light, any kind of light. Because for me, that means hope. And that's what I need at this time. Hope.

In-Laws

Some people can't stand their in-laws. Some people can't live with them, not even for a second. After what happened in my life, I quickly found out that I can't live without them. If you look up the definition of the perfect grandmother, you'll find a description of my mother-in-law, Barb. She has been unbelievably helpful since it happened, since I lost my wife, since she lost her daughter. She has committed herself to helping me take care of my children, and she also takes care of me. She watches them during the day while I'm at work, and she even stays most evenings to help out with them after I get home. She's great with the kids. She's a former teacher, and you can tell when she interacts with them. She talks to them, holds them, and loves them like only a grandmother could, like only a grandmother should. Catherine's sister, Sandy, has also been amazing. She took a leave of absence from work for several months to help out with the kids. She's also been great with them and a tremendous source of support. Without my in-laws' love, their strength, their devotion, and especially their help with my children, I'm not sure where I would be right now. I'm pretty sure I'd be more lost than I already am. They have both helped provide a path toward normalcy, a path toward healing.

In My Life

There are places I remember
All my life, though some have changed
Some forever not for better
Some have gone and some remain
All these places had their moments
With lovers and friends I still can recall
Some are dead and some are living
In my life I've loved them all

But of all these friends and lovers
There is no one compares with you
And these memories lose their meaning
When I think of love as something new
Though I know I'll never lose affection
For people and things that went before
I know I'll often stop and think about them
In my life I love you more

Though I know I'll never lose affection
For people and things that went before
I know I'll often stop and think about them
In my life I love you more

In my life I love you more
(Beatles)

Inside Jokes

Ever turn to someone—not just anybody, but the person you love—and say something silly, something seemingly meaningless yet somehow unbelievably humorous? That was my existence with Catherine, inside jokes. Sometimes no words were even spoken. Sometimes we would just glance at each other, just give each other a look, and we would completely understand the situation, the irony, the nonsense. Mostly, we would just say a word, a phrase, and one of us would always finish the other one's sentence. Then we would just look at each other and laugh. Laughter—that is definitely one of the things I miss the most. We had so many good times together, so much happiness, that it's almost painful to even remember. Not because they were bad times; it's because I know they will never come again, at least not with Catherine. Those moments are irreplaceable. Just like my wife, irreplaceable.

Irony

Irony is being a physician, being a cardiologist, and having two infant children less than two months of age, less than four pounds in size, on blood pressure medications. I spend the majority of my day—actually, every day—treating hypertension (high blood pressure) and writing prescriptions for my patients. Now I have to give both of my kids blood pressure medications twice a day, the very same medications I usually prescribe. It's actually a little ridiculous. I have to draw up tiny amounts of a liquefied medication in a miniature syringe and shoot it into their cheeks. Then I have to quickly force a pacifier in their mouths so they instinctually suck down the medication into their system. At least the medication is mixed with some sort of sugary substance so they don't actually hate it, but it just doesn't seem right. It doesn't seem natural. And, well, it really isn't, when you think about it. Infants shouldn't be on hypertension medications. Checking an infant's blood pressure is not exactly easy either. Whenever the nurse visits or when I take them to the doctor, my kids really don't appreciate a tiny BP cuff inflated on their arms or legs. Some adults almost cry when I do this, so an infant would obviously not enjoy the process.

The doctors say hypertension is a common problem for preemie infants and they should eventually outgrow it, whatever that means. I've said similar things to patients, not in exactly the same vein and not really pertaining to the treatment of hypertension, but similar enough to not get my expectations too high. It's been over eight months, and I still find myself giving both of my kids tiny doses of that same liquefied medicine, with no relief in sight. It's not like I can offer my kids the same advice I usually give my patients. I can't exactly have my kids exercise more and avoid fried foods. I can't tell them to stop adding salt to their food, like I tell my patients.

Another ironic twist to my so-called life is the fact that my son, Declan, needed heart surgery one month after he was born. He had a patent ductus arteriosus (PDA), which is just a fancy medical term for a heart problem very common among premature babies. It's a problem where abnormal blood flow occurs between two of the major arteries connected to the heart. Without getting into too much detail, it ended up being a major problem for my son, which is an understatement. His first month of life was a real struggle, to say the least. After several weeks, he just wasn't getting any better. The doctors really didn't want him to have heart surgery because of the risk of the anesthesia and the operation, so they delayed it as long as they could. They kept trying medication to circumvent the problem, but I knew better. It got to a point where I insisted he have the operation to fix his heart because he just wasn't thriving, he wasn't even growing.

So he underwent heart surgery. He actually sailed through the operation and ended up doing very well in the short-term. Then the following night came. That's when he crashed. That's when we almost lost him. Before my wife died, I would have to say the longest night of my life was the night after Declan's surgery. He couldn't breathe on his own, and he was critically ill. The worst of it was, since I was a physician, I actually understood how sick he was. I knew how close we came to losing him.

Catherine was beside herself. It really bothers me to remember how upset she was, how much pain she was in that night. I felt so helpless the night my son almost died. Sort of like how I feel now, helpless. Because despite all my knowledge, all my medical training, I couldn't physically help my son. He was sick, so very sick. Catherine and I stayed by his incubator all night long, weeping, teary-eyed. We held each other because we couldn't hold our son, he was too ill. As the night gave way to the day, and as the sun slowly began to rise, my son slowly got better. Every day since that surgery, he has gotten bigger, he has gotten stronger. The problem now is that Catherine is no longer here to witness his growth, his progress. Although I couldn't be happier for my son's health, I couldn't be sadder that he will grow up without a mother. Both of my children, Declan and Violet, will never know the most important person I have ever met. They will never know her love, her warmth, her strength, her humor, her intelligence, her care. They will never meet my better half, my love, my Catherine.

Joy

This is something I am sorely lacking. I readily admit it. I've got little to offer, little to share, when it comes to joy. I'm all stocked up in other places. I've got plenty of sadness. I've got a car stockpiled with Kleenex boxes. I've got a broken heart full of despair. I've always been full of something. At least, that's what Catherine would often say about me with a soft smile and a knowing look, that I was "full of something." But when it comes to joy, that's definitely missing.

It's an expected consequence of what's happened to me. It's no surprise; in fact, it's just reality. But day after day, week after week, month after month, it wears on you, an entire life, an entire existence, without joy. That's just too much for anybody to bear. Since April 2012, that's what my life has been. Empty, joyless. The supposed happiest moment in your life should be the birth of your children. But when my kids were born, they were whisked away in seconds to the NICU and placed on respirators because they couldn't breathe on their own. So it's been a rough ride; it's been a long year.

I've gotten to the point where I feel like I've reached rock bottom. It sounds cliched, but it's true. You always hear the saying "It could always be worse," and of course, it could be. But I think I've reached the end, at least I hope so, and I tell myself that. It can't get any worse; I've been through too much. So I now try to find joy in my life. Not every day—I'm not nearly that rehabilitated, not that positive. But I still try to search for it, mostly through my kids. I see joy and happiness in their eyes. They're so young, so innocent. I see them smile, and I find joy through them. That's what keeps me going. That's why I get out of bed every morning—for my kids, their lives, and my life I can share with them. Because that is what it's all about now, really. My kids. When you get past everything else in the world—possessions, material things, everything—when it comes down to it, there's nothing else that really matters but your family. And that's what joy really is, at least for me. That's what I have left, my kids. I'll do my best to take care of them and find joy in my life through them.

Kangaroo Care

For the first couple of weeks, they didn't even seem real. My kids didn't seem real. They were so small, so paper-thin that you could almost see their hearts beating in their chests. You could definitely count their ribs while the machine they were hooked up to pumped oxygen in their lungs. The worst part was, we couldn't even hold them. They were too sick, too unstable at first for us to take them out of their prison, their little incubators.

After a few weeks, after they got a little bigger, a little stronger, we were finally able to hold them. The hospital actually had a name for this, for the time you were able to take sick, premature newborns out of the incubator: kangaroo care.

Catherine loved kangaroo care. It was finally real then. It was meaning-ful. To hold your own kids, to actually interact with them, was amazing. Mind you, we could only hold them for thirty to sixty minutes at a time because they weren't big enough to regulate their own body tempera-tures, but it was still priceless. I remember taking turns. I would have kangaroo-care time with Declan, and Catherine would hold Violet, then two days later, the earliest we could take them out again, we would switch off. I remember the first day Catherine held both of them at the same time. It was kind of a mess with all the wires, probes, and oxygen lines hooked up to both of them and Catherine in the middle, holding both of our children. I remember how happy she looked, her smile. But her eyes told a different story. Her eyes showed suffering, that she felt pain because of what the twins were going through, what they had already been through. Her eyes, they made me hurt, because I knew. I could tell how hard this was on her and on me.

I have pictures of Catherine and our kids during kangaroo time. I've looked at them only once since she passed away. It hurts too much. It pains me to remember how she smiled while holding them, yet how much she suffered back then. It also bothers me to remember how sick my kids were, how small and vulnerable they were. I try to focus on them now, and they both seem to be doing well. It's unclear what the future will bring for them, how they'll turn out. All I have to hold onto these days is hope. For the sake of my kids, I hope they will grow up healthy. They have enough problems to deal with al-ready, and they are not even ten months old yet. They won't have a mother to grow up with, and that's a big enough problem for them—and for me.

Kleenex

A few days after Catherine died, I felt trapped. I was free in a physical way, but I was almost struggling to breathe. Mentally, I was in prison, with a life sentence. I was at home, surrounded by friends, family, in-laws, and my two children. There was constant motion, almost chaos, in my mind, along with constant tears and never any silence or alone time. I decided I needed to leave. I had no idea where I was going to go or what I was going to do, but I had had enough.

I checked on both of my kids to make sure they were OK and told my brother I was headed out. I remember looking at him, probably with dead eyes, and saying, "You're in charge. I'm going for a drive." My mom was there, and, of course, she was worried. But I told her I was all right, though in reality, things were pretty far from being OK. How could I be all right just ninety-six hours after my wife hung herself?

As I gathered my shoes and sweatshirt and made a beeline toward the garage door, somebody handed me a box of Kleenex. I stopped in my tracks and looked up. Anna, Catherine's best friend, looked at me with what I saw was pity, although it probably was just compassion, and said, "Here, take this for the drive."

It didn't even register at the time. Nothing did. I just blindly took the box of Kleenex and headed out the door. At the time, I really had no idea where I was going. I just needed to leave. I threw the Kleenex in the passenger's seat. Nobody was going to sit there anytime soon anyway, and I pulled out of the driveway.

The only place I could think to go was the Starbucks down the street. It was sort of comical, in a way. In my darkest time, my time of need,

I found myself turning to absolute commercialism and big money for comfort. I guess that says a lot about me, and our society. Well, I had no intention of hanging out there comparing notes on the newest dark-roast coffee beans, so I grabbed a cup of joe and headed back to my car. As I slid behind the wheel, I figured out the obvious. I realized why Anna had given me the Kleenex because I just doubled over, right there, in all the glory of the Starbucks parking lot, and emptied my soul. I must have sat there and cried for a while because I soaked up Kleenex after Kleenex in stride, and my beloved coffee actually cooled down to a reasonable drinking temp.

After a little bit, I gathered myself and checked my surroundings. For some reason, I wanted to make sure no one was watching, which is kind of silly. Who would be at Starbucks watching some poor guy basically lose his shirt in his car?

As I started my car, I had no idea where I was going to go. But as I pulled out of the parking lot, I finally realized what I had to do. I headed to the cemetery, where the day before I had picked out the plot to bury my wife. I'd sprung for the double plot, so there was room for me when the time comes. As I pulled into the cemetery, I felt a little ridiculous. I was going to stand in the middle of this cemetery and stare at a plot of ground where I would soon bury my wife. But for some reason, it just felt right.

I parked my car on the side of the road and just sat there. I let the engine idle, listened to some mindless music on the radio, and thought, "How in the hell did I get here?" The truth that reality presents is almost impossible to comprehend unless taken in context. If you'd suggested that one day I would be sitting in my car, listening to music in the middle of a cemetery, my only company a fresh box of Kleenex sitting next to me, I would have said you're crazy.

But there I was. Alone in a cemetery. I snagged another handful of tissues and got out of the car. I headed up the small hill toward my dead wife's future gravesite. I was careful not to step on anybody's plot on the way up. I weaved between various headstones—some new, most old—and sat down under a tree. I had picked my wife's resting spot under a large tree, and for some reason, it seemed appropriate. It seemed right. It's hard to explain why; I guess you can't really relate unless you have buried a spouse or loved one. I sat there and stared at the ground. I tried to think of all the wonderful times we had shared together. But I could only think of the dark times over the past several months. The endless days in the hospital, visiting our kids. The times at home when Catherine would sit and worry about our kids, about their health, their lives, their futures. I sat there and wept, with nothing to wipe my tears away but Kleenex. At least I was prepared.

From that point on, I never left the house without tissues in the car. While I'm writing this, it's been almost seventy days since Catherine passed away, and I have gone through three boxes so far. It's not like I sit there and bawl my eyes out the whole time I'm in the car. But I do have a few meltdowns as I drive. It's probably because driving in my car is my only alone time each and every day, my time to think, reflect, and, most importantly, remember. I obviously only try to focus on the good times, but I often drift back toward the dark times. But overall, I think it's helpful. It's a healing process, as painful as it may be. It may not work for everyone, but it's a part of my new routine. A routine with my new companion, a fresh box of Kleenex, which never judges, always offers comfort, and never lets me down.

Labor and Delivery

Everything will be OK. Those words haunt me to this day. Sometimes—well, quite often—I speak those words silently to myself while I'm driving or when I'm in bed staring at the ceiling, struggling to find peace within myself, waiting for the sun to rise. It's because those were the exact words I spoke to Catherine when she went into labor at twenty-seven weeks, six days, a far cry from the forty weeks of pregnancy any obstetrician would advise.

She was in the hospital, on bed rest, for nine whole days before she went into labor. When I wasn't at work, I was beside her at the hospital the entire time. My routine back then was to come straight to the hospital after work, spend the night, go home in the mornings for a quick shower, and then head off to work. Set and repeat.

For the first week, everything seemed OK. Catherine's contractions had slowed down, and I was actually a little optimistic. But Catherine wasn't; I could see it in her eyes. The last night before she gave birth was the worst. Her contractions became more frequent, almost every five to ten minutes, and panic set in. She kept looking at me for help, for guidance, for a solution. I can't tell you how helpless I felt; it was so defeating. It was painful because I make my living in health care. My job description is to help and care for people, but all my knowledge, all that medical expertise, was useless at this point. Being a cardiologist afforded me no further advantage or help in this situation over someone not in the medical field. In all the time I'd known Catherine, I'd always been able to guide her through difficult moments, no matter what they were. But not this time, not now. As they wheeled her off to the labor and delivery floor, she looked at me and cried. Through streaming tears, she said, "It's not going to be OK. It's not. The kids won't be all right."

All I could do was hold her hand in mine and offer my love, my support. That's what I did when I said, "Everything will be OK." Over and over again, these words run through my mind. At the time, I truly believed that sentiment. And as far as my kids are concerned, for now it does appear to be true. It hasn't come easily for them, as they both spent months in the hospital. But now they're both finally at home and seem to be doing well.

What I struggle with is that it wasn't true for my wife. It wasn't true for Catherine. Things quickly went from bad to worse after she was transferred to labor and delivery. A team of specialized doctors, neonatologists, waited for us there. They had nothing good to tell us; they absolutely crushed our spirits. They spoke to us in quiet monotones, describing all the terrible things that could go wrong with our children, how they could be permanently disabled, both mentally and physically, and how there was a chance they wouldn't even make it out of the hospital alive. I can remember holding Catherine's hand while they spoke to us, almost down to us, telling us these horrible things, and feeling as if the world was going to end. The birth of your children is supposed to be the single most important life-changing event, the happiest moment in your life. Instead, pain and misery surrounded us. I understand why they told us what they did. I get it because I'm in the medical field. But it's different when you're on the other side. It's different when you or a loved one is a patient.

Catherine was only in labor for about four hours before she delivered Declan. He was born at 4:11 p.m. on May 10, 2012, at two pounds, five ounces. I remember crying at his birth. He was incredibly small, ridiculously small; he almost didn't seem real. He was so thin, so tiny, so helpless. He didn't even look like a baby. He gave out a short, weak whimper, and then they whisked him away to the NICU, putting him on a respirator to keep him alive. After he was born and Catherine was stabilized, the doctors saw that my daughter wasn't ready to be delivered. Catherine's contractions had slowed down tremendously, so they attempted to wait it out and not deliver my other child. It was such an odd feeling to know that your wife had been pregnant with twins, yet only one child was delivered and your wife was brought back to her room. The doctors thought that the longer they kept my daughter in utero, the better off she would be. I immediately asked how often they had tried something like this before, and the doctors responded, "It's not very common." But they provided an anecdote of a few years ago when they had delivered twins a week apart to afford the second baby a few more days of development.

Well, like everything else about our experience and Catherine's pregnancy, that plan didn't quite work out. A few hours later Catherine went into labor again, and they moved her back to the delivery room. Fortunately, she didn't require a cesarean section, and Violet was delivered at 9:53 p.m. the same day at two pounds and ten ounces. Like Declan, she looked incredibly small, incredibly helpless, and they immediately took her away to the NICU to help keep her alive.

I remember looking at Catherine at that moment. She appeared exhausted, even too tired to cry. In the span of five hours, she had undergone two separate deliveries and was deprived in both situations of seeing her children because they were too small and too sick to even allow her to hold them. I felt so helpless, so lost, but I did the only thing I could do at the time. For the second time that day, I took her hand in mine and spoke the same words that eventually proved to be so untrue that they haunt me to this day. I said, "Everything will be OK." In the end, it wasn't. Not even close. Not for her, and not for me.

Last Christmas, 2011

No, this isn't a tribute to Wham's classic holiday carol, although I shamelessly admit that I do love that song. This is, in fact, a reference to the holidays, specifically the last Christmas Catherine and I spent together.

It's definitely true what people say—the holidays are tough sometimes. They are especially difficult when a loved one dies, when your wife dies. They are tough for all the obvious reasons. The holidays are special times, at least they are supposed to be. It's when you spend a little more time with your family, with your friends. It's when you create new memories, reminisce over old ones, and look forward to the coming year. I was fortunate to have spent seven wonderful Christmases with Catherine as her husband and many more before we were married. They were memorable; they were all special in their own ways. But it was last year, last Christmas, that I remember the most.

It was about a year ago that we first found out Catherine was pregnant. At first, we didn't tell a soul. We talked about it and planned on telling Catherine's parents on Christmas Eve. So, per our routine, we headed over to her parents' house that day. I wanted to let her tell them, so I spent the entire day waiting for Catherine to spring the big news. All through dinner and into the evening she said not a word, offered not even a hint, until we sat down by the tree to open some presents, another holiday tradition for our family.

After a few presents were passed around, Catherine opened a small Christmas-ornament picture frame. It had two slots for tiny pictures of our smiling faces to hang on the tree for years to come. After Catherine opened this gift, she turned and smiled at me and then abruptly said, "Well, next Christmas it'll be plus one." That's all she said, sitting there under the tree with such a beautiful grin on her face. Her mom looked at her, confused for a moment, and I said, "She's pregnant. There'll be another one around the tree next year." It was only "plus one" at the time because we didn't know that she was pregnant with twins. We also had no idea what 2012 would bring.

I look back upon our last Christmas with mixed emotions. I smile when I remember how happy Catherine was, how excited she was to start a family. But I also feel pain, almost unbearable hurt, because of what happened, because my wife isn't with us, with our kids, to share their first Christmas. As the holidays draw closer, I'm doing my own math, my own calculations. I start with "plus two" because of the twins. But after I factor in what happened with my wife recently, I also have to "minus one." And there you have it. That about sums it up for my family this year and for years to come. Minus one.

Last Time I Saw My Wife

It was a typical morning, a typical day. I followed my old-faithful routine, no deviations, no changes. We both slept in a bed in the nursery with our kids. I woke up that day at 5:30 a.m., after a few short hours of sleep. I leaned over and woke Catherine up, and I went downstairs to make up the bottles for our kids. When I came back upstairs, Catherine was changing Violet's diaper, as she usually did. I handed her Violet's bottle and scooped up Declan, who was still resting nicely. I proceeded to change his diaper, and Catherine sat down on our large, white beanbag chair and began feeding Violet. I took my usual place in the rocking chair and fed Declan. I remember distinctly that it was a good morning. Both our kids ate well. No fuss, no crying, at least at that point. We both finished, and Catherine brought Violet back to our bed to hold her up. Violet was spitting up quite a bit back then, which, I guess, is an understatement. She was spitting up a lot, and the trick was to hold her upright for about an hour to help her digest her bottle. This sometimes worked and sometimes didn't. Either way, Catherine always held her in her arms after each feeding. I put Declan back in his crib, jumped in the shower, and got ready for work.

As I came back in to the nursery to say good-bye, Catherine was lying down with Violet on her chest. Both cats were also in the bed, snuggled next to her. Catherine looked so beautiful that morning; she looked perfect. She held Violet with such loving arms while the baby rested her head on Catherine's chest. As I walked over to the bed, Declan starting wailing in his crib. I turned around to pick him up, and Catherine said, "Put him in the bed. He'll be OK." I said, "Are you sure?" After she smiled at me, I placed Declan in the bed next to his mother and commented, "Everybody's in the bed. One big, happy family." I bent down and kissed both my kids and then kissed Catherine good-bye. That's the last time I saw my wife alive, in our bed, smiling, surrounded by our two children and two cats. One. Big. Happy. Family.

Life and Toothpaste on My Butt

Losing your wife when you have two children changes everything. That's obvious. My life is completely different now. How I view things, how I interact with my patients, my friends, my family—everything is just different now, and it hurts. As the days go on, as time passes, I slowly realize how devastating this really is. The big things in my life—my children, finances, hiring a nanny—are obvious new changes, and I am trying to cope with this. However, the little things also take their toll.

For example, part of my morning routine is that I brush my teeth in the shower. I know, I know, most people probably find this disgusting. The funny thing is, so did Catherine. But it didn't bother her too much because we used separate showers. I sort of rationalize the act by telling myself it saves time, but I do realize it is sort of gross.

Well, a few days ago I put a gob of toothpaste on my brush, turned, and stepped in the shower. After I flipped on the faucet, I looked down; my brush was empty. No toothpaste. Nothing on the shower floor, nothing on my feet. I even looked outside the shower on the bathroom floor and couldn't see where the toothpaste had fallen. At the time, I just assumed that it fell right down the drain. Though that really didn't seem like a plausible explanation, I wasn't in the mood to dwell on this at six in the morning. So I finished getting ready for work (I had to brush my teeth after I got out of the shower, and I hated it!) and went to the office.

At the end of the day when I left the office to go home, I opened my car door and stared at the seat. There was this chalky, blue/white substance all over my seat, sort of pasted on. It took all of five seconds to make the connection. That morning when I had turned to get in the shower, the toothpaste must have fallen onto my scrubs laid out next to the sink. I must have been so tired that after I got out of the shower I didn't even realize I'd put on pants with a huge gob of toothpaste on them. I then knew what I would see before I even looked. I turned my head and saw the same chalky, blue/white paste all over my ass. I'd walked around all damn day with my butt fit for a dental office, and nobody had had the decency to tell me.

At that moment I thought about telling Catherine what had happened. About how ridiculous it was to work a full day in the office and have nobody tell me about my toothpaste butt. I got in my car and cried. I realized that I couldn't share this stupid, ridiculous thing that had happened to me because she wasn't here. It's not like I wanted to go home and tell my mother-in-law about this. I guess I could have. But, number one, it's not the same. And number two, it is kind of embarrassing to admit to people that I brush my teeth in the shower, because it's gross. So I drove home in tears, thinking about this and all the other experiences in my life—both meaningful and meaningless (like today)—that I can't share with Catherine because she's dead.

That's the point. That's another reason for my emptiness, for my pain and sadness. Life is more than the big things. Life is about everything. It's important to share even the most mundane and silly experiences with someone. At least it is for me.

Moving forward, I'll do my best to brush my teeth and not cover my ass with toothpaste, because I have no one to share that story with either.

Life Insurance

Suicide doesn't pay—another bold and provocative statement from yours truly, Captain Obvious. But it's true. It's just another one of a million things I'd never thought about or didn't have to deal with until my life changed forever. To be honest, I didn't even know that Catherine had life insurance through her employer. I certainly had a policy in my name, but that's what you're supposed to do when you're married and you have kids. I'd actually increased my benefits two weeks after I found out Catherine was pregnant. But I had no idea that she also had a policy. Not that it was anything special. It was a small, basic plan offered by her law firm as a standard part of the benefits she had signed up for when she was hired. Not that it even matters now, because suicide pretty much null-and-voids any standard life insurance policy, which makes sense if you think about it. Her claim is actually still pending, and it's been over a hundred days since she passed away. I am extremely grateful to Catherine's law firm for even attempting to file the claim and offer up a fight, but I'm not counting on receiving any benefits. Trust me, I could certainly use the money. I would try to pay down my mortgage and save a good portion for my children's college education. But I'm not expecting anything. Because nobody benefits from suicide. The people who are left behind are in pain, just as I am in pain. No amount of money could ever take that pain away, because what I said earlier is true. Suicide doesn't pay.

Lost

Sometimes I feel lost, just totally lost. Not in a physical sense, just emotionally and mentally lost, which is probably a lot worse. There's no Google Maps or GPS to help me find my location, let alone where I need to go. I guess that's what happens when you lose your best friend, when your wife dies. It's literally like losing yourself, or at least a part of you. I've lost the best part of me. I had known Catherine for almost half my life before she passed away. I met her when I was eighteen years old and she died forty-three days shy of my thirty-sixth birthday. It's actually hard for me to remember my life *before* I met Catherine. All my memories, at least my good ones, involve the times we spent together. And now she's gone.

I find myself thinking of what I should do next. Not that I have any pressing matters, but it's like I lack direction. I understand my purpose; trust me, I clearly do. My life, my goal, my purpose revolves around

67

raising my kids, and I'm doing the best I can. But I still feel lost. I think it's because I feel alone. Well, I am alone. It's not like I can talk to my wife about the do's and don'ts of raising our kids, because I can't. I know, I can clearly talk with my mother-in-law, my nanny, my friends, and even my pediatrician. But it's not the same, and you know this. It's hard to describe, but I truly feel lost sometimes.

I know the basics, and that's the easy part—changing diapers, bottle-feeding (clearly not breast-feeding), and holding my kids. I obviously have that down by now. It's the big picture that's missing here. Parenting styles, discipline, raising my kids—it's all on me now. I never thought I would be in this position, alone, raising two kids. There's no manual, there's no book, not even a good reality television show I can DVR. I know I'm not the only single parent who's ever crossed this barrier, who's ever raised kids alone. But it's still fairly uncommon for a single father to raise kids. Think about it. If you're still reading this, ask yourself, how many single fathers do you know? And being divorced doesn't count. If you can't think of many, you're not alone, because it's pretty damn uncommon.

I'm not writing this for pity or sympathy. I'm just telling you how I feel, being honest. I think about this and I feel lost at times. Being a single father scares me, it really does. I have a daughter, and I have no idea what to do with her. I can't help her with makeup, I can't help her with clothes, and I certainly can't help her with dating advice. I know, I know, it's years away, but it still doesn't change the problem. I'll do the best I can (insert any cliché you like), put one foot in front of the other and move on. But it still doesn't change the fact that I feel lost.

Maybe one day I'll find a path. Who knows where it will lead? As long as my kids are on that same path and are healthy and happy, I'll be OK. That's all I ask for now, for my kids to grow up happy, and I'll do the best I can. That's not too much to hope for, is it?

Making Headlines

A few weeks ago, I came into work and found the local community paper on my office desk. Upon closer inspection, I saw that the front-page headline was a story about a cardiologist who had saved a heart attack patient by putting two stents in one of his coronary arteries. In the bottom right-hand corner of the paper, there was a picture of a guy who looked just liked me, except he didn't. He looked a few pounds heavier, though he had my beard. He grinned, almost a smirk. But his eyes, his eyes looked different. They were clear and brown, hopeful eyes, much different than mine. They didn't appear sad at all. I hardly recognized myself.

Looking past the picture, I realized what this was all about. Several months ago the local hospital where I work wanted to publish a brief article spotlighting a cardiologist and a story about treating a heart-at-tack patient. I had completely forgotten about this, you know, given the fact that my wife had died. After reading the first couple of paragraphs, I remembered the patient and what had happened. The incident dated back to the spring and had occurred when Catherine was on bed rest. I remember the night distinctly, like it was yesterday. My pager had gone off and I'd immediately known what it was about. I'd hated leaving Catherine that night, even though it was going to be just for a few hours. She wasn't technically sick at that time. She was quite stable, still at home, and not having contractions—yet. I still hated leaving her, but I had to go to work. I remember leaving for the hospital and returning a few hours later and Catherine was still up. She said she had just woken up, but I knew better. She had been up the whole time, worrying, being scared, and I hated that.

After reading the article, I didn't know what to do. My first instinct was that I wanted to tell Catherine about it, I wanted to show her the piece. In the scheme of things, this wasn't a big deal. When I say that this was in the local paper, I mean it. It wasn't *USA Today* or the *Wall Street*

Journal; it was the local community paper. But like anything else in life, it's nice to be appreciated at times. I'm not really into awards and recognition, but I'm still human, and it was nice. Like most people, I don't live in a vacuum. Well, I used to not live in a vacuum. My point being when something happens to you, good or bad, you want to share that something with somebody close to you, be it your parents, your sibling, your best friend, or your spouse. And that was the problem. I completely realize that this was a very small ordeal, nothing notable at all. Still, I wanted to tell my best friend about it. I wanted to tell Catherine about it, and I couldn't. That's something I'm going to have to live with for the rest of my life. All my successes, all my failures I have to hold onto myself, alone. I won't be able to share them with my wife, with my best friend. These are the things I've come to realize, things that I'm going to have to accept. And that's it, that's life.

Well, maybe one day I can share this silly story with my children. One day when they're older, much, much older, I can tell them that their old man was a physician, a cardiologist, who actually took care of patients, who helped people. Here was proof, legitimate proof, printed in the local community paper. So I took that paper home with me after work and put it in my desk drawer at home, in a safe place. It's just too bad the picture they used in the article doesn't match me completely. It's not a true representation. Maybe one day I'll look like that cardiologist again. Maybe one day my eyes will match that picture and not be so sad.

Midnight the Cat

One day after I got home from work, Catherine was changing Declan's diaper. She turned and looked at me with a big smile and said, "Saw Midnight today." Of course, she was referring to our neighbor's big, black cat named Midnight. It was a very appropriate name because our neighbor's cat was jet black. The babies' changing table is in front of a window that faces our neighbor's yard, and Catherine must have seen Midnight playing outside that day. From that day on, every time I came home from work I would ask Catherine if she'd seen Midnight. Sometimes I would ask as soon as I came home. Sometimes I would forget and ask right before we went to bed. But no matter when I brought it up, she would always answer with a smile. Truthfully, she rarely saw Midnight. It was only on occasion, but I still loved to see her smile when I asked.

These memories all came back to me the night after Catherine died. After all the commotion had died down, I found myself changing Declan's diaper at the very same changing table, and I happened to be in the room by myself. I looked out the window at my neighbor's yard and whispered, "Did you see Midnight today?" to an empty room, except for my infant son, and I proceeded to break down. It was all I could do to finish changing Declan's diaper without collapsing into oblivion. I realized I would never see Catherine again. I would never see her beautiful smile, and I would never be able to share that moment with her again.

It's been fifty-six days since she passed away as I am writing this, and to this day I have difficulty changing my children's diapers at that changing table. I always find myself looking out the window at my neighbor's yard, searching for Midnight, searching for answers, searching for anything that can take away my pain.

Mother's Day

Sunday, May 12, 2013. Mother's Day. It's a date, like many others, that I am now dreading. I know the first few years won't be that tough because my kids are too young to understand. For now, that's a good thing, because I'm definitely not ready to begin to talk about what happened to their mother. Eventually I will be. I know I will tell them at some point, because it's the right thing to do. But for now, I'm not ready.

I've thought long and hard about what I should do on Mother's Day, and I've come up with the idea of taking my kids to the zoo. It was actually a recommendation from a friend. It could be the start of a new tradition, part of my new routine. Catherine always loved animals, and I think it would be nice for the kids. They'll probably be a little too young at first, but as the years go by I think they'll appreciate it. At least I know I will. It can be a relatively decent distraction, which is what I think I'll need moving forward. It will also provide a little happiness for my kids. Every small child loves the zoo. It's an indisputable fact. Well, at least that's what I tell myself, because I really don't know what I'm doing. But I'm doing the best I can, and I think that's what I'll plan for this spring. As long as the weather is nice and it's not pouring down rain, I'll pack up some formula, a few diapers, gather up my kids, and head to the zoo. At the very least, I will get to see my kids smile. And at this point, that's the only thing in my life that makes me smile.

Money

Just because your heart is broken, it doesn't mean it stops beating. Just because you feel like your life is over, it doesn't mean you don't continue to breathe. And just because you feel like your world is going to end, it doesn't mean the sun won't come up the next morning.

That's what I had to learn, that's what I needed to accept, as painful as it was. I took about two weeks off work after Catherine died, but I eventually needed to go back. I needed to leave my self-made cocoon of sorrow. I had to make money again; I had to earn a check, not to mention the fact that I went from a two-income household to a single-income family in the blink of an eye. I had a mortgage to pay for, school loans I couldn't ignore, bills to mail out, and two very tiny mouths to feed.

So I dried my eyes, even if was only temporary, ventured forth, and went back to work. To be honest, it wasn't easy. It was downright painful at times. But I needed to do it. My kids needed me to provide for them because I was all they had left. And you want to know the truth, the honest truth? If it wasn't for my kids, if I wasn't a father, I may have given up. I might have considered cashing in my chips and moving. Blowing off my responsibilities and taking some real me time. Just leaving town with no direction, no purpose, and no future.

But I'm glad I didn't. I'm glad I've picked myself back up. I come home from work every night, look at my kids, and smile. It almost hurts to smile. After months and months of shedding tears, of constantly being sad, it really does hurt sometimes to smile. But I can't help myself. I hold my kids and smile, because they possess the best of their mother, the best of Catherine, and hopefully the best of me. And that's all I have left, which I realize is more than some people. So I cherish my kids. I live for them. I work, I pay my bills, and I try to save for their college education. Not because I need to, because I want to. No matter how sad I get, how upset I am at times, I look at my kids and quickly find a reason to get up every morning. I find a reason to move on, to live, because being a father means something. At least it does for me.

Music

"All by Myself," Eric Carmen
"Stairway to Heaven," Led Zeppelin
"If I Could Turn Back Time," Cher
"I'm So Tired," Beatles
"Just When I Needed You Most," Randy VanWarmer
"The Living Years," Mike + the Mechanics
"Throwing It All Away," Genesis
"Sad Eyes," Robert John
"What About Me," Moving Pictures
"All Out of Love," Air Supply
"Biggest Part of Me," Ambrosia
"Baby Come Back," Player
"Tupelo Honey," Van Morrison

"Never Let You Go," Third Eye Blind
"Haven't Got Time for the Pain," Carly Simon
"Let It Be," Beatles
"If You Leave Me Now," Chicago
"You Don't Know How It Feels," Tom Petty
"Love Bites," Def Leppard
"No One Is to Blame," Howard Jones
"Don't Forget Me (When I'm Gone)," Glass Tiger
"Goodbye Girl," David Gates
"Pick up the Pieces," Average White Band
"The Tracks of My Tears," Smokey Robinson and the Miracles
"Woman," John Lennon
"Over the Rainbow," Judy Garland
"Too Late for Goodbyes," Julian Lennon
"Leaving on a Jet Plane," Peter, Paul and Mary
"It Had to Be You," Frank Sinatra
"Into the Mystic," Van Morrison
"It's Too Late," Carole King
"It Don't Come Easy," Ringo Starr
"Right Down the Line," Gerry Rafferty
"Don't Dream It's Over," Crowded House
"Dig a Pony," Beatles
"I Don't Want to Live Without You," Foreigner
"You're My Best Friend," Queen
"I Can't Hold Back," Survivor
"With or Without You," U2
"King of Pain," Police
"Two of Us," Beatles
"Missing You," John Waite
"Rainbow Connection," Kermit the Frog
"You Are My Sunshine," Rice Brothers Gang
"Changes," David Bowie
"Shattered Dreams," Johnny Hates Jazz

"You're the Only Woman (You & I)," Ambrosia
"One (Is the Loneliest Number," Three Dog Night
"Alone Again (Naturally)," Gilbert O'Sullivan
"I Love You," Climax Blues Band
"The Sound of Silence," Simon & Garfunkel
"I Need You," America
"Poor Poor Pitiful Me," Jackson Browne
"You Are the Woman," Firefall
"Dust in the Wind," Kansas
"You Can't Always Get What You Want," Rolling Stones
"Every Breath You Take," Police
"Still the One," Orleans
"Endless Love," Lionel Richie and Diana Ross
"Reminiscing," Little River Band
"More Than I Can Say," Leo Sayer
"Need You Tonight," INXS
"Only the Good Die Young," Billy Joel (Different context, but never-
theless true.)
"So Far Away," Carole King
"Photographs and Memories," Jim Croce
"Keep on Loving You," REO Speedwagon
"Dream Weaver," Gary Wright
"Total Eclipse of the Heart," Bonnie Tyler
"I Guess That's Why They Call It the Blues," Elton John
"Coming Around Again," Carly Simon
"I'll Sleep When I'm Dead," Warren Zevon
"Knockin' on Heaven's Door," Bob Dylan
"Never Gonna Fall in Love Again," Eric Carmen

My Love
I've been through so many changes in my life, woman
It's a wonder I ain't lost my mind

And I ain't never said how much I need you, sugar
But I sho' need you by my side

My love, just thinking about you baby
Just blows my mind
My love, just thinking about you baby
Just blows my mind all the time

You've been my friend and you've been my love, oh Lord
Honey, you're everything I need
You've made my love so strong, now I know where I belong
Oh girl, you'll never have to worry
Oh baby, anymore, anymore
(Lionel Richie)

Nanny

I hired a nanny about two weeks after Catherine died. I had to go back to work; I had to make a living to support my family. I knew I couldn't function effectively if I was up all night with my kids. Plus, it wouldn't be fair to my patients, not to mention myself, to be constantly sleep-deprived. It wasn't like I was sleeping well at night anyway, but I had to at least give myself the opportunity to sleep.

So that's what I did. I interviewed several nannies and finally picked one I liked, a very sweet lady, somebody I felt I could trust. But the first night she came, the first time I handed over my kids to her and shut my bedroom door to make a useless attempt at sleep, I cried. And I couldn't stop.

All I could think about was Catherine and how she never wanted a nanny. She wanted to take care of our kids herself, with my help, of course. It shouldn't be this way, I thought. I shouldn't be handing my kids over to a stranger because my wife killed herself. I shouldn't be alone, a single parent, a single father.

I didn't sleep that night, not a minute. But I've kept my nanny, and she's been great, she's been wonderful. The kids seem to like her; that sounds foolish because my kids are so young, but they really do seem to like her. As the nights pass and the days go by, I've learned to sleep a little. Not always through the night, and not always restfully, but I at least have the opportunity to sleep if I can. That's something I need, my patients need, and most importantly, something my children need if I'm going to be able to take care of them.

Neonatal Intensive Care Unit (NICU)

"When is your due date?"

That was the question posed to us by the physician, the premature baby specialist (neonatologist), approximately seven hours before Catherine gave birth to Declan on the morning of May 10. At the time I thought the question was ridiculous because the doctor obviously knew the answer. Catherine had been in the hospital on bed rest for over a week at that point. She was constantly surrounded by doctors, and they obviously had read her chart. But I'm, unfortunately, familiar with this game. Anytime you ask a question you already know the answer to, you are either trying to prove a point or reinforce an existing one. So Catherine told her August 3, her due date.

Our neonatologist responded, "Well, that's about how long you should expect your kids to be in the hospital. You both have to understand that your children will probably be hospitalized until then. That's the expectation."

That's when the bottom dropped out and despair set in, because it was at that moment that we realized our kids would be sick enough to require hospitalization for eighty-five days, the exact number of days until her due date.

That was our welcome to the NICU. "Here is the tour of our unit, and, by the way, this will be your children's new home for the next eighty-five days. Enjoy your stay..." The sad part about it was that they were pretty damn accurate. Violet was in the hospital for seventy-six days, and Declan was held captive for ninety-one days.

The days in the NICU were the hardest. Those were the darkest times in the hospital, by far. I can't describe how difficult it is to see your kids in incubators, so small, so helpless. Hooked up to breathing machines because they aren't strong enough to take breaths on their own. Connected to lines and IVs, attached to feeding tubes. The worst part was not being able to touch them, not being able to hold them in your arms, to tell them it was going to be OK. That was the worst. It took several weeks before we could take them out of the incubators on a daily basis. Even then, we could hold them for only a short time before we had to put them back. They were so small, so young, yet they still cried when they felt pain, when they hurt, which, unfortunately, was quite often. They had their blood drawn on a regular basis. They underwent procedures, had IVs placed, were examined, poked, and prodded. It was just a living nightmare. I've heard parents talk about how miserable it is to watch their kids get vaccinations, and I just sort of chuckle. Not because it's untrue, because it actually is, but because it can be so much worse, so unimaginably terrible, people can't even fathom it.

All this wore on me. And it obviously tore up Catherine, emotionally and mentally. Day in and day out, we were both in the NICU, we were both at the hospital. Catherine bore the brunt of the torture because I had to go back to work. But Catherine, she was at the hospital eighteen hours a day, every day. She was always there, by our kids' side, every day. I can't imagine how she did it. I still can't. I would work during the day and then go to the hospital in the evening, so I was only there four to six hours a day, and that was incredibly painful. It was difficult to see my kids sick, helpless, especially as a physician, somebody who'd spent his entire life learning how to help and provide medical care for others, yet I was unable to help my own children. That was brutal.

But Catherine was at the hospital every day for ninety-one days in a row. I can't tell you what kind of toll that took on her, what kind of pain she must have endured. Although she never admitted it to me, I know she felt guilty for what had happened, even though she shouldn't have. That just compounded the pain; it multiplied the suffering.

Although our kids slowly got better and slowly got stronger, Catherine never really recovered. She never really got better; she never really got stronger. She was too proud to show it and too proud to admit it, but she was obviously in pain. Knowing now how much pain she must have been in continues to haunt me, continues to keep me up at night. It is this pain I must learn to accept and must learn to live with. The only problem is, I'm not sure I can.

Never Be The Same

And I'll never be the same without you here
I'll live alone and hide myself behind my tears
And I'll never be the same without your love
I'll live alone and try so hard to rise above

The years go by
There's always someone new
To try and help me forget about you
Time and again, it does me no good
Love never feels the way that it should

I loved you then, I guess I'll love you forever
And even though I know we could never stay together
I'll think of how it could have been
If we could just start all over again
(Christopher Cross)

New Shoes

It has probably been over ten years since I've bought any article of clothing for myself. It's not like I have been wearing the same shabby clothes for over a decade. I actually probably would be, but Catherine always seemed to buy me whatever I needed, or more precisely, whatever she thought I needed. The funny thing was, she was always right. I would come home from work, there would be a box on the kitchen table or in the living room, and she would smile and say, "Open it up." There would always be a nice pair of shoes or a sweater or some jeans or a new coat. The thing of it was, whatever she bought me was perfect. That was Catherine; she not only had impeccable style, but she also knew what I liked. She was also clued into whatever I needed. She would spot holes in my socks or T-shirts, and the next day there would be new socks or T-shirts waiting for me.

That brings me to now. My work shoes, which, naturally, Catherine had bought me last year, were starting to look pretty ragged. I wear the same shoes to my procedures in the cath lab, and over time they inevitably get covered in blood. I know I can always use shoe covers; however, for some reason I never liked putting those hideous "hospital blues" on my feet. I even clean them off from time to time but they still take a beating, literally.

Over the past several months, I began to notice that my shoes were in pretty bad shape. Since Catherine was no longer around to take care of me and buy me new shoes, I knew I had to move on, be a grown-up, and take care of the problem. I know this probably sounds a little ridiculous, making a big deal about buying new shoes. But for me, whose old routine meant Catherine would always be there to take care of things, it's hard to start over, to start a new routine. But that's what I did. I logged onto the World Wide Web, remembered the various brands of shoes Catherine had always picked out for me, and promptly bought myself some new shoes. New shoes that will take me in a new direction, put me in a new routine. Just another part of my life that's different now, and will always be different.

Nights Are Forever Without You

Lying in bed with the radio on
Moonlight falls like rain
Soft summer nights spent thinking of you
When will I see you again

Curtains still dance with the wind and the sky
The sun will be coming up soon
But I just can't sleep for thinking of you
Here alone with the moon

Soft and low the music moans
I can't stop thinking about you
Nights are forever without you
Nights are forever without you
(England Dan & John Ford Coley)

Obituary

CATHERINE LYNN BECK (nee Bucher), aged 35 years, passed away Sept. 27, 2012. Dearly beloved wife of Agustus A., loving mother of twins Declan Alexander and Violet Alexandra, cherished daughter of Jerry and Barbara (nee Siers) Bucher, devoted sister of Sandy Vazquez. Funeral service Wednesday, Oct. 3, 2012, at the funeral home at 2 p.m.

Burial following in Lake View Cemetery. Family will receive friends to pay tribute and celebrate the life of Catherine at the DeJohn-Flynn-Mylott Funeral Home of South Euclid, 4600 Mayfield Rd. (just east of Green Rd.), Wednesday, 12 noon until time of service.

Published in the *Plain Dealer* from September 30 to October 1, 2012.

Operator (That's Not the Way It Feels)

Isn't that the way they say it goes
Well, let's forget all that
I've overcome the blow, I've learned to take it well
I only wish my words could just convince myself
That it just wasn't real
But that's not the way it feels.
(Jim Croce)

Outnumbered

I have always felt that life is like a numbers game, and the name of the game is to not be outnumbered. At least, that's how I have viewed things. For as long as I can remember, I never wanted to be outnumbered, which is a little weird to write on paper, because who in their right mind wants to be outnumbered? But I have oversimplified this and applied this to my life and my household.

It started over ten years ago, shortly after Catherine and I first moved in together. At that time, we had two cats. Catherine would jokingly ask about getting a dog, or even another cat. My response was always "We can't be outnumbered. We'll lose the power," referring to the number of animals in the house. I never wanted more animals than adults, more pets than us. That's why I always put my foot down at two pets.

As an aside, I didn't want a dog either because we were not home enough. Growing up with a dog as a pet, I learned that it wasn't fair to have one unless you could be home all the time, at least that's how I feel. Cats are a different story. They are self-sufficient, to say the least, and sometimes like being by themselves anyway.

A few years ago, Catherine read online about a family that kept a hedgehog as a pet. For some strange reason, she became fascinated with the idea of having a hedgehog. I don't really know how serious she was about the idea, but I always came back to the numbers game. I insisted we couldn't have more than two pets, and since we already had two cats, game over.

Well, this also carried over to the idea of starting a family. Thankfully, Catherine and I were definitely on the same page about this, regardless of some silly mantra about being outnumbered. We had always agreed on two kids. Naturally, it seemed like a blessing when we found out she was having twins because we would be done. We would stop at two, and everything would work out perfectly.

Needless to say, this didn't happen. Kind of the understatement of the year. Now I wake up every morning and feel outnumbered. Now that Catherine is gone, I feel so alone. I have two children, and it's just me to raise them. I'm obviously not literally alone; my in-laws have been great and help out with my kids *every* day, but you know it's not the same. My comical rule about not being outnumbered has been shattered, along with all the dreams Catherine and I had together. I am left with the task of trying to bring order to my existence. Order to and control of my life, my kids, and my sadness. Hopefully, one day I will. Through the love I have for my children, I will try my best, but the truth of the situation never escapes me. It's because life always comes down to a numbers game. I have two children, and they have one parent. Outnumbered.

Packing Away Her Life

Two weekends. That's all it took. Two long weekends to pack up her clothes, her shoes, her purses, all her belongings and put them away. I don't know if that speaks to my efficiency or if it's more a sad commentary on life. I like to think it's the former, but it's probably more of the latter.

I decided shortly after she passed away that I didn't want to look at her closet anymore. I want to remember her, and I obviously think about her all the time, but for some reason I didn't want to see her clothes hanging in the closet anymore. I actually gave most of her belongings away to Goodwill. I kept a few nice things, some of her purses and most of her jewelry, for Violet. Her sister, Sandy, helped as well and sold some of Catherine's things on consignment. But mostly, I gave a lot of her clothes to charity.

Really, when you think about it, belongings are just material items. Sure, some hold sentimental value, but I feel the most important things to keep, to cherish, are my memories. Although I packed away Catherine's belongings, I've maintained my memories, my experiences. I'd spent essentially half my life with her, and you can't pack that away. That's impossible. So although her clothes, purses, shoes, and jewelry are stowed away in my attic, and the rest are on some shelf in a Goodwill store, my memory of her is kept locked away in my heart.

Patience

You need a lot of patience to raise a child. You especially need a lot to raise twins, and you need even more patience when you have premature infants. Unfortunately, patience isn't a commodity you can buy. It isn't something you can just stock up on, although I wish you could. I wish you could just flip a switch or push a button and refill your patience tank. This would be especially useful when my kids are crying, when they lose it. If you are a parent or surrounded by infants or babies in any capacity, you understand. There are essentially two types of tears when a baby cries. There's the regular crying when babies are hungry or they want to be picked up. And then there's total insanity. That's when your child is completely inconsolable, no matter what you do. You can hold them, change them, feed them, try to play with them, and nothing will work, nothing will stop their tears. That's when my patience runs out. That's when I close my eyes and envision an internal gauge where the needle approaches empty. That's when I feel like giving up, especially when both of my kids are losing it at the same time.

Believe it or not, this is when I try to think of Catherine. I think of how patient she was with our kids. How she spent hours upon hours at the hospital sitting with them every day. How she held them and took care of them after they were finally discharged. That's when I try to refocus. That's when I try to refill my tank and not lose my patience, because I owe it to Catherine, to myself, and to my kids to be as patient with them as I can. Moving forward, I promise myself that I will do the best I can and try to be a strong, caring, and patient father.

Patients

My patients have been great. Their support and goodwill have really helped me through this process. They have taken care of me just as I have spent time over the years taking care of them. It's definitely been the best part of my job. There is a downside to being emotionally vested with your patients, though. It sometimes offers a constant reminder, sometimes prevents me from truly escaping, from really being distracted from my life, from my situation, which is what I need at times. Trust me, I don't blame any of my patients for anything they say or ask me. But it's still hard, it's still very difficult to be asked certain questions, to be constantly reminded.

Meeting new patients is sometimes tougher. That's because I'm often asked if I'm married or if I have any children. I'm still not comfortable answering those questions; I probably never will be. I just usually answer, "No, I'm not married" and "Yes, I have children. I have twins." But the downside to being truthful is that my response usually invites a slew of other questions that are also tough for me to answer.

I have realized one bright side, one small difference since my life changed. I find myself being more empathic with my patients, a direct and obvious consequence of what I've been through, of what I've experienced. I can now honestly relate to my patients who have experienced a loss, who have undergone their own personal tragedy. This may seem like an inconsequential benefit, but I don't think so. I think it has made me a better doctor, for what it's worth. Having an empathic doctor is not the norm, at least not in our society.

So I try to look at the positives in my life, even if I have to force myself, even if they are few and far between. I have realized that living through everything I have gone through over the past ten months has changed me. That is undeniable. Living through these experiences—seeing my own children sick and in the hospital for months, having almost lost my son after his heart surgery, and actually losing my wife to depression—has changed me forever. And if it has made me a better physician, then I'll take it. But I also hope I can be an even better person, a better father to my kids, because I will need that strength to move forward, to continue to live.

Paris

Catherine always wanted to go to Paris. She didn't talk about it much, but when she did, I could tell she really wanted to go. I could see it in her eyes. So after a little convincing, we packed our bags and went to Paris for our fifth wedding anniversary. It was our last big vacation together, our last big trip, which is rather unfortunate because, at the time, we thought we had a whole lifetime together. We both thought we had several decades to take vacations together. And why wouldn't we believe that? We were both young, healthy, and in good spirits. More importantly, we were in love.

Our time in Paris, for the most part, was excellent. We were only there five days, but it was just the right amount of time. We spent the days sightseeing, and we saw the usual suspects. We went to museums and hit up the Louvre for a day, though you could actually spend an entire week there if you wanted to. We saw the Pantheon, the Tuileries Garden, and, of course, we went to the Eiffel Tower. My only complaint about the trip was the language barrier, the inability to communicate if you can't speak French, which neither of us could. Catherine was a little overzealous and bought the French Rosetta Stone education DVDs, but she never really got very far before our trip.

In the end, we survived the language difference and had a wonderful time, not just because we were in Paris, more because we were together. I'd rather have great company versus a good destination. I would rather be with someone I truly care about, I really love. I've always been that way. When you can have them both—great company and a great destination—then you're set for a perfect trip, a perfect outing. Catherine and I could have gone anywhere for our fifth wedding anniversary and I would have had a great time. That's something I can't replace, that's one of the many reasons I've been in so much pain, I've been so lost since she died. Catherine is irreplaceable, plain and simple. Moving forward and living my life—going on trips, vacations, having time off—will never be the same. My life will never be the same because great company always trumps a good destination. No matter where I find myself, I will be alone. I will be without great company. I will be without my wife, Catherine.

Philosophy 101

I wish this section were about great philosophical advice, sage wisdom I would personally use and could also share to help others. But it isn't. It is actually the class I took the first semester of my freshman year in undergrad. It was in this class that I accidentally, and not so graciously, introduced myself to Catherine.

This was back in 1995, a lifetime ago. And the exact details of the class topic or my conversation with the professor has long been forgotten. But I do remember the context, to a point. The professor was a young postgraduate student who I could tell was a little apprehensive, a little insecure. I also remember disagreeing with the topic of the day's lecture. For some reason that day—and truthfully, I was probably just being inappropriately brazen—I raised my hand and began to argue her point. I basically questioned the very heart of her lesson plan. And the funny thing was, I think I was right. I think my argument actually held some water and I had correctly questioned the professor. It was sort of like the scene from the movie *Old School* when Will Ferrell surprisingly dominates James Carville during a debate. Well, it wasn't quite that dramatic, but it still made quite an impression on the professor, so much so that she actually threw up her hands in disgust, canceled class, and ran off the stage in tears.

Now what follows I am not terribly proud of, but let's be honest, I was eighteen years old back then and a lot less mature, a lot less sensitive. After I basically made the professor cry and cancel class just ten minutes into her one-hour-and-fifteen-minute lecture, I stood up and high-fived the guys sitting around me. There was actually a small cheering section near me for getting the class canceled. Well, Catherine was also in that class, which I didn't know at the time, and, frankly, I probably wouldn't have cared if I had known. I remember Catherine telling me later that that was her introduction to me, that that was basically how she met me. She pretty much thought I was an immature punk, and, honestly, she was probably spot on.

After that little incident, Catherine didn't really make it a point to hang out with me. I don't blame her. I remember seeing her on occasion over the next few years, mostly because we had mutual friends in common. As time passed, we slowly became good friends, which is a little surprising given how she first met me. Toward the end of our senior year in undergrad and leading into the summer, we started to date. A few years later we got married, and the rest is history.

Catherine was right. I was basically a punk back then, back when I was eighteen years old and just a kid. But I have, thankfully, outgrown that mentality and matured immensely, with Catherine's help, I might add. Before she died, I would often look back at that time and marvel at the story of how we first met, of how Catherine first saw me in action. I am living proof that first impressions don't always stick, that people can change. I have changed. Truthfully, I owe a lot of who I am to Catherine. Without her in my life, I know I would have turned out differently, most likely for the worst.

Moving forward, I will never regret the fact that Catherine was in my life. Despite the pain, despite the tragedy, I'm a better person for having known Catherine. I also still have the best part of her in our children. At least that's what I see when I look in my kids' eyes every night when I get home from work.

Pictures

I found them. Her pictures. Her photographs. I wasn't even necessarily looking for them. It occurred by accident. About two weeks after it happened, there was a postcard addressed to her in the mail with a coupon for 20 percent off all digital photographs. That's when I remembered all the pictures she had taken and collected over the years. I had forgotten she had uploaded them to an online photo website years ago.

I took the coupon and went upstairs to my computer. Although I appeared calm, my heart raced. It took a few attempts, but I eventually figured out her password and logged onto her account. I was instantly overwhelmed. There were hundreds of photos. I suddenly felt the pain and sorrow well inside me, ready to burst through. I slammed my laptop shut and went back downstairs to feed my kids, attempting to bury my sadness deep within my soul. Although I knew this was impossible, I just couldn't handle looking at those pictures then. I wasn't ready, and at the time, I felt I would never be ready.

Well, I finally looked through those photos. Not all of them, but most of them. About three months later, I was driving home after what seemed like an impossibly long day at work. As the snow fell and I drove through the darkness, my mind betrayed me, as it always does. I was thinking of Catherine, remembering her, missing her, basically keeping my wounds fresh, feeding the embers of my sorrow. For some reason, I thought of her online photo account. I decided to look at her pictures.

I pulled off to the side of the road about one block from my house and took out my phone. Although I had my heater on full blast, a chill went down my spine as I logged onto her account. Like ripping off a Band-Aid, an impossibly large Band-Aid, I slowly swiped through our life together.

There was a decade of happiness in those pictures. Photos from school, of graduations and weddings, from the beach, vacations, and holidays gone by. Photos of her family, of us, of our cats, of our lives. I looked at them through tear-filled eyes. I slowly swiped through each picture, pausing only long enough to catch my breath and admire Catherine's beauty. Her smile, her eyes. I had forgotten her eyes, how pure, how happy she had looked back then. Although I'd lived with her and seen her every day, I hadn't seen those eyes in months, not since she was put on bed rest. Not since our lives were derailed had I seen such happiness, such joy in her eyes.

I sat in the dark in my car on the side of the road and cried. I cried for my loss. I cried for my kids. But mostly, I cried for Catherine. I cried because of her eyes. I cried because of how much pain she must have been in before she died. She was such a vibrant, happy person before our lives were turned upside down, before our kids were born prematurely, before they spent months in the hospital. She would never show it. She would never let people know how upset she was, how tormented she was. But if you knew her, if you looked into her eyes, you could tell. You could see the pain in her eyes. I knew, but I obviously didn't know the extent of her pain. I cried that night for her.

I eventually gathered myself, used my trusty box of Kleenex that I now always keep in my car, and drove the final block to my house. Then I turned the switch. I made the change. I wiped away the last tears from my eyes and walked into my house to see my kids and greet my in-laws. I can't tell you how hard it is to flip the switch, to turn off the sadness and put on a smile. I do it every day, for my family, for my in-laws, for my patients, and especially for my kids. I have to stay positive, at least when I'm around my patients and my family, and it's not easy. I just hope that one day I won't need the switch, I won't need boxes of Kleenex in my car. I just hope one day my eyes will match Catherine's in those photos. I hope one day I can be happy again, even just for brief moments.

Pride

I've always had pride. It's something I've carried with me for as long as I can remember, for better and worse. I also know it's a quality that's carried me through to where I am today. Catherine had pride as well. It was one of the many things I loved about her, but it also didn't serve her well in the end. She was often too proud to ask for help because she thought she could always just figure it out and do it herself. She was talented, ever so talented, and she often didn't need any help. She often thought she could do things better than anybody else anyway, so what was the point in asking for assistance?

You know, I wish she would have let somebody in, let somebody help us in the end. We interviewed several nannies to help us take care of the twins after they finally came home from the hospital. Frankly, I didn't like most of the nannies. However, there was one I felt comfortable with, which says a lot because I think I'm pretty particular myself. But Catherine didn't like any of them. There was always something wrong with each nanny, with each individual we interviewed. Too old, too young, too inexperienced, too shy, too talkative. In reality, we could have interviewed Mary Poppins and Catherine wouldn't have been happy. She always felt she could take care of our kids better than anybody else, even if it was by herself. I admired the hell out of her for doing this, and maybe it was my fault for not pushing harder to hire some help. But she seemed like she was doing OK, and I was doing the best I could to help when I came home from work. I got up with her at the 2:00 a.m. and 6:00 a.m. bottle-feedings, changed my share of diapers, and helped around the house. Even to this day, when I look back, I don't think I could have done any more than what I did. Maybe I'm just convincing myself of that, but I don't think so. At least I tell myself that.

This brings me to today as a proud single father taking care of newborn twins. Well, I quickly got a taste of reality shortly after Catherine died, and I let my pride go by the wayside. It was about forty-eight hours after Catherine had passed, and it was two thirty in the morning. I was up trying to bottle-feed both of my kids, not coincidentally because I couldn't sleep anyway. I was alone in the nursery, feeding Violet while Declan cried in his crib. It was a pretty low point for me. I felt hopeless, lost, and alone. It was at that point I realized I had to hire a nanny, that I had to let go of my pride and ask for help because I certainly needed it. Reality has a funny way of setting in and pushing your preconceived ideals and notions to the wayside. Sort of like that quote from *Pulp Fiction* when Marsellus Wallace is talking to Butch about fixing the boxing match: "The night of the fight, you may feel a slight sting. That's pride f*cking with you. *F*ck pride*. Pride only hurts. It never helps. You fight through that sh*t."

Well, my position wasn't as dramatic or exciting as that, but from that moment on I changed my routine and I started asking for help. This, coming from a guy who never asked for help, ever, as long as I can remember. But I knew what kind of predicament I was in, and I was honest with myself. In order for me to successfully raise my children as a single father, I needed help. Thankfully, I'm surrounded by a wonderful group of family and friends who've been able to get me through this.

Questions?

If it wasn't for the questions people ask, work—well, life for that matter—would be much more tolerable. The constant barrage of questions that come my way on a daily basis wear on me. In my line of work, I encounter several different people every day. Most, if not all, know what has happened to me. And they ask questions, all day, every day. I get questions from nurses, techs, other doctors, and, especially, my patients. To them, to the world, I've become "that guy." You know, "that guy" who has experienced something tragic, something terrible, whom you talk about with your friends and family because it's uncommon, it's something different, because the world, our society, is fascinated by tragedy. They want to know what happened and how you responded. Let me tell you something intuitively obvious, you never want to be "that guy." You don't want to be the person whom a coworker or friend goes home and tells his wife or her husband about. You don't want to be the topic of discussion at someone's dinner table. You don't want to be "This guy at the hospital where I work had twins who were born three months early and were sick for months. Then his wife was obviously depressed and killed herself. Terrible. Just awful."

Once you become "that guy," a person of interest, you have to answer questions. You have to satisfy people's curiosity and shoulder their sympathy, even their pity. I remember having a conversation with Catherine when our kids were still in the hospital. She had no interest in talking with other people. She was actually terrified of it, so she turned off her social clock. She didn't want to discuss what had happened to us, what had happened to our kids. I know a part of it was that she felt guilt, which was obviously misplaced, but that was how she felt nonetheless. She also said something I will always remember. She was scared of how people would look at her, at how people would treat her. She didn't want anybody's pity. She was too proud a person for that. She was scared, actually terrified, that if she started talking to her friends, she would see or hear their pity. She couldn't take that, so she shut everybody out. Since the time she delivered until the day she died, she shut everybody out of her life except me and her parents. She obviously didn't share everything with me as well, including her guilt and pain.

I can relate to her feelings, to a point. Especially now, since I've become "that guy." I definitely don't want anybody's pity, but I also don't enjoy answering everybody's questions. I try to use work as a distraction—as a way to forget about my life, about my dead wife—and focus on taking care of my patients. But the questions people ask offer a quick reminder of my situation, my empty existence, my pain. I don't blame people for asking me, I really don't, but I still don't like to hear their questions.

"How are you doing?"

"How are the kids doing?"

"How much do the kids weigh now?"

I do the best I can with my answers. I keep them short and full of cliches. Normally I hate cliches, but I can't think of anything else to say. I certainly can't tell people the truth. When it comes down to it, people really don't want to hear the truth. They don't want to hear that it's a struggle to breathe, that I'm in constant pain. They don't want to hear that I often lie awake all night long with nothing but my own tears to keep me company. People don't want to hear that when morning finally comes, I struggle to get out of bed. They don't want to hear that I hurt so bad some days that I actually feel physically ill. Some days I feel so much despair, so empty, that I feel nauseous. I feel sick.

So when it comes down to it, I tell people what they want to hear.

"I'm doing the best I can."

"I'm taking one day at a time."

"I'm focusing on my kids." (I actually am, but this also sounds so cliche to me that I hate saying it.)

Either way, I've accepted the fact that I will always be "that guy." I was definitely a person of interest after my kids were sick and in the hospital for several months, but I've reached legendary status after my wife killed herself. I realize the questions and concern will eventually dissipate and taper off. But one thing will never change. For as long as I live, I will always be "that guy," and that makes me sad. This is exactly what it means when I tell people that I'm different now. My wife's suicide, her tragic death, is and will forever be a part of me. For most people, when they sit down at the dinner table and tell a story about a guy they work with, they are not only fascinated with what happened, but deep down they're happy as hell that they are not "that guy." Because being "that guy" sucks, and I wouldn't wish that upon anybody.

One day, maybe, "that guy" will actually be able to breathe again without struggling. Maybe he will be able to sleep at night. Maybe he will be able to drive home from work without sad eyes filled with tears. Maybe he will be able to look at people and smile a real smile, one that isn't forced. Maybe "that guy" will be able to answer a question without lying. Maybe "that guy" will be able to turn and look someone in the eyes and tell them, "I'm doing OK; I'm fine" and actually mean it.

Routine

Your life is your routine. Your routine is your life. Think about it; it's true. You do the same thing every day, day in and day out. That's your routine, that's your life. Even if you say you do something different every day, that's still your routine. That's your expectation, doing something different day in and day out. Your routine can change, but your life also changes, it evolves. You grow up, go to school, make new friends, date, get a job, start a career, move, get a new job, marry, start a family, have kids. Every step of the way, every milestone, you form a new routine and stick with it until something changes, until you need to evolve.

The secret, the lifelong plan, is to find a routine that not only works for you but that you also love. I had that once. I'm not saying my routine, my life, was perfect, but that's not the point. I was once happy with my routine, with my life before Catherine died. You might find that hard to believe after what you've read so far, knowing what I've been through with my kids being sick, in the hospital, but it's true. My life, my routine, has been turned upside down. It has changed immeasurably over the past year. But it was my life and my routine, and I was happy. Don't get me wrong, there were plenty of dark times, plenty of sadness. But I coped with it. I changed my routine, and I moved on, partly because I was optimistic, partly because my two kids got better. They slowly, but eventually, got healthier. But I coped mostly because of Catherine. She was with me every step of the way, by my side, guiding me through my life, my routine. Going to the hospital every day to see my kids was almost unbearable, but I was able to do it because Catherine was with me. She was there to support me, and I was there to help her. We had each other. That was my routine. That was my life, intertwined with Catherine's, and with the addition of our two kids, Declan and Violet.

Now that Catherine is gone, now that she has passed away, I feel lost. I feel empty. I haven't given up; I just have to form a new routine. But it's different now. I'm different now. I still get up every morning like I used to. I still make my coffee and go to work just as I have always done. But now when I leave the hospital, when I'm done with work, I come home to a different house. I come home to a different life, a different routine. Instead of coming home to see my wife, to see Catherine, I come home to my in-laws. They're at my house helping me take care of my kids. It's great that they are willing to help me, willing to be a part of my life and my children's lives, because I don't think I would have been able to cope without them. But it's not the same. It's not the same as coming home to see Catherine in the living room holding Violet, Declan lying on the couch next to her.

So that's the problem. That's the struggle, living with and moving forward with my new routine. I know I have to. I don't have a choice, I have to take care of my kids. I plan on doing this to the best of my abilities and with the help of my in-laws, Catherine's parents, Barb and Jerry, and her sister, Sandy.

But the problem now is my sadness, my emptiness. I've come to realize—and, unfortunately, accept—that this is my life now. This is reality, and it saddens me. It does. To come to the realization that my life, my routine, is always going to be half empty because I feel half empty, is sad. But I haven't given up hope, because without hope, why move on, why live? I do hope that one day I will incorporate some happiness in my life, in my new routine. That's my goal, that's why I still get up every morning. And I hope that I can find this happiness with my children. I hope they grow up healthy and I can one day become whole again. At least that's the plan, that one day I will be whole again and happy with my life, my new routine.

Sad Eyes

People's eyes are very telling. You may not notice, but if you pay attention, you can tell a lot about how someone is doing by just looking into their eyes. I quickly realized this through my patients. I interact with several patients every day, and I try to do my best to put up a front. I want to make my patients feel comfortable and confident in my abilities as their doctor, so I don't want to walk into their rooms with a sad demeanor. That wouldn't be fair to them. So I try to stay upbeat and positive when I talk with them. All of this is not easy, by the way. It can be downright impossible at times, but I do my best. It really is the only thing I can do at this point.

I'm not always successful. Last week while I was rounding at the hospital, I saw one of my patients of about two years, a very nice elderly lady who was admitted with chest pain and had suffered a small heart attack. I explained to her that she was doing well and was very stable. As I turned to leave, she stopped me and said, "Doc, you have very sad eyes." It was more a statement of fact than anything else. I was completely taken off guard by her sentiment. She could see right through my smile, my handshake, my bedside manner, and noticed the pain in my eyes.

I have tried to use that experience as a lesson, or at least motivation to try to heal. I'm not even sure how that is possible, but I am going to do my best. Not just for me, but for my patients, my family, and most importantly, my children. I don't want to raise kids with sad eyes. I don't want them to grow up and see me in pain all the time. How can I raise happy and healthy children if I don't heal myself? Well, I don't know. But I hope I can one day look in the mirror and see different eyes looking back at me.

Sadness

It's hard to pinpoint what triggers my sadness, my pain. It can be a song on the radio, a commercial on TV, a conversation with a patient, a photograph, or a memory. It can come from nowhere, or everywhere. I can be going about my day, distracted, working, and, *boom*, it can hit me like a ton of bricks. Total sadness. Enough to take my breath away. Enough that I have to seek refuge, that I have to escape, that I have to find an excuse to go to the bathroom where I can cry in silence, alone with nothing but my thoughts and tears to keep me company.

However, there is one particular thing that really bothers me, really upsets me. It's when I see other families together. It's when I see a mother pushing a stroller, taking a walk with her child down the sidewalk. It's when I see both a mom and a dad at the end of the driveway, waving good-bye to their son as the school bus drives away. It's when I see a little girl whisper into her mother's ear at a table in a restaurant. It's these moments, these particular times, when I weep, when I just can't seem to hold it together. It's because I know my kids will never have those moments, and countless others, to share with their mom, to share with Catherine. I know there's nothing I can do, and that's the point. I don't have an answer, and I never will. Catherine's gone, and I have accepted that, but it's so damn hard to live with. Especially when I think about our kids. When I think about Declan and Violet growing up without a mom, it hurts, it really does. I just hope the sadness and pain dull a little over time. It's been eighty-five days since she died, and it hasn't. Not even a little.

Sailboat

I have always appreciated art, but I have never collected any pieces, nor would I know where to begin. Catherine always had a better understanding of art. She would always bring up the fact that she took an art class in college. The few times we went to an art museum, she quickly displayed her knowledge. And truthfully, it was impressive. But I never really let her know I felt that way. I would always tease her about it, asking impossible questions about certain paintings and then responding, "What, they didn't teach you that in Art 101?" She would sort of laugh, playfully so, and often come back with a wittier remark about one of my many shortcomings.

I was never one to look at a photo or painting and picture myself in the art. It's an interesting exercise, and I'm sure there is a more technical term for this practice, but I'm not sure what it is, probably because I never took an art class.

I found myself at work the other day looking at a painting of a sailboat. There was a medium-sized sailboat by a dock floating on a crystal-blue lake in the middle of a summer day, the kind of day where you can see for miles with only a few clouds in a sea of blue. Seven chubby little pigeons all facing different directions wandered around in disillusionment on the pier. They were the kind of birds Catherine would appreciate. I found myself looking at the boat and picturing me and Catherine on its deck, sailing to the middle of the lake, which is ridiculous because neither of us was capable of sailing a boat. But Catherine would sometimes talk of owning a boat one day and learning how to sail. She would mention it from time to time, especially when we were on vacation. It was just something silly people say when they dream. Not that dreams are silly, but they are often overlooked and never accomplished. I looked at that picture and started to cry because I knew all of Catherine's dreams were over, silly or not. All of her plans, all of her goals, and all of her love—gone.

I couldn't take looking at that picture anymore. I walked away feeling sad and thinking about how my life has turned out, thinking about my dreams. Right now, thinking about the future is pretty tough. It's hard to have dreams when your life gets turned inside out and upside down.

I do hope that my kids will grow up healthy and be OK. I dream that maybe one day I can take them sailing, just the three of us. Maybe it will be a medium-sized sailboat floating on a crystal-blue lake in the middle of a summer day. Maybe I'll look up into the sky and see blue for miles with only a few clouds. Maybe I'll point at the nearby pier and show my kids the chubby little pigeons all facing different directions. Maybe I'll tell them how they are birds their mother would have liked. Maybe.

She's Gone

Everybody's high on consolation
Everybody's trying to tell me what's right for me
My daddy tried to bore me with a sermon
But it's plain to see that they can't comfort me

Sorry, Charlie, for the imposition
I think I've got it, got the strength to carry on
I need a drink and a quick decision
Now it's up to me, ooh what will be

Up in the morning look in the mirror
I'm worn as her toothbrush hanging in the stand
My face ain't looking any younger
Now I can see love's taken her toll on me

Think I'll spend eternity in the city
Let the carbon and monoxide choke my thoughts away
And pretty bodies help dissolve the memories
But they can never be what she was to me

She's gone
(Hall & Oates)

Social Security Office

I had no idea I was eligible for spousal death benefits. Death benefits are not something you really think about or discuss with your spouse when you're in your midthirties. But things are different now. Shortly after Catherine died, her law firm's human resource department contacted me regarding the benefits I should look into.

Well, it appears that if your spouse has paid any money into the social security system, and assuming that social security is not bankrupt by the time you read this, you are entitled to death benefits if:

1. You have children under the age of eighteen years old.

2. You have children over the age of eighteen years old and they are disabled.

A few tips about dealing with social security. I will just relate my experiences with my adventure to the office. I looked up the business hours of the nearest office; they happened to open at 9:00 a.m., so I decided I would get a jump on it and arrive about fifteen minutes early. As I drove by at around 8:45 a.m., about ten to twelve people were already standing in line outside the building. Better yet, when I pulled into the parking lot, there were no spaces left. I did an eight-point turnaround because the lot was so small and proceeded to drive around the block looking for a place to park.

Now, mind you, this particular office is not located in the best part of town. Geographically speaking, it is close to the east side of town, which is not the best side to be on. I finally found a reasonable parking spot on the street where I didn't think I would be carjacked, and I walked about two blocks back to the office. By the time I arrived, there were sixteen people in line and just about everyone looked unemployed and disabled. At that point I probably fit right in because this was about one week after Catherine passed away and I was in my parachute-pants-and-T-shirt phase, so I didn't exactly look like a model citizen either.

I waited abut twenty minutes in line before I could actually get into the building, shuffling along slowly, passing empty double-deuce beer cans and cigarette butts tossed outside the building. As I entered, I quickly realized I was in trouble. It was like a clown room— forty people inside this impossibly small space, basically on top of each other. The room appeared smoky, and the lighting was a terrible off-white/yellow florescent glow that made everything just a little too dim, but unfortunately not dim enough. The walls and ceiling were painted yellow as well, and there was a tall man standing up front handing out numbers. Next to him were about four rows of five chairs each, all jammed with people waiting desperately for their number to be called, yet the office had just opened minutes ago. Behind the rows of chairs were two small bank-teller windows and yet another line of people waiting to be helped. It didn't make any sense. It looked like more than thirty-five people were jammed in this fourteen-by-twelve-foot, tiny room, and what I couldn't possibly understand was that this office had just opened *twenty-five minutes ago*!

I had the privilege of getting into another line just to meet the tall man who appeared to be running that day's show at the social se-curity office. As it became my turn to take the next number, the man handing out the golden tickets asked me what my purpose was, like I had nothing better to do than hang out on a Tuesday morning with these people in this crowded and smelly room. I looked at him with dead eyes and barely whispered that I was there to talk about spousal death benefits as my wife had just passed away. He then gave me a curious grin and asked if I had an appointment, as if he knew that I didn't. When I told him that I, in fact, did not have an appointment, his curious little grin slowly exploded into a nice, big, sh*tty grin and he said, "Well, you'll have to wait about nine hours then,"

I didn't even break stride and promptly responded, "You guys are only open for six and a half hours today." The God's honest truth, his great big smile got even a little wider when he said, "It seems you have a problem."

Unbelievable! I just looked back at him, not letting him see my feelings of disbelief, and stared into his eyes for what must have been another thirty seconds, not saying a word. I realized that this *sshole was not about to give in and offer any semblance of advice, let alone sympathy for the death of my wife. I broke the silence by asking him if I could make an appointment. He then pointed to the left where there were two very tiny windows, the bank teller windows, past a row of chairs all filled with sad, seemingly destitute people. He said I could wait in that line, but that we'd probably "have lunch together" before I would be able to make an appointment.

I wasn't about to wait another three hours in this crappy hole, next to this jabroni, while he continued to take pleasure in other people's misery. I responded with the only logical question left: "Is there a phone number I can call to make an appointment?" He then pulled a small stack of papers out of his pocket, ripped the top piece off, and handed it to me without breaking his grin. It read SOCIAL SECURITY, followed by an 800 number. As I turned to leave, I could hear my friend ask the poor guy behind me, "Sir, do you have an appointment today?"

I walked back to my car, head down, defeated, and drove home. I ended up calling that number and waited on hold for thirty-five minutes before I could actually talk to a human being and not a recording. The problem is there appears to be only one number to reach social security for the entire nation; there are a lot people in our society, and there's only *one* number. I ended up making an appointment for the following week and wisely picked another location that was a little bit farther from my house but in a more reasonable neighborhood. Plus, I couldn't handle going back to that same office for fear of seeing my friend again, smiling and grinning, torturing people with his appointment question.

My next encounter with social security went surprisingly well. I did a little online research and brought the appropriate documents. For those inquiring minds, you need your birth certificate, your social security card, your children's birth certificates/social security cards, your spouse's certified death certificate and last two pay stubs, the previous year's W-2 tax returns, and a copy of your marriage license. Got that? You basically need to bring with you a small binder of documents to accomplish anything.

All in all, the appointment took about forty-five minutes, and I starting receiving benefits for my children three weeks later, benefits I have used to fund 529 college savings plans for both my kids. Also, I did receive a one-time payment of two hundred fifty-five dollars for a spousal death benefit, which I thought was pretty random. I am not exactly begrudging this payment—it was used to buy diapers and formula for my children— but I just thought it was a strange amount. Apparently, it's a standard benefit when your spouse passes away and is technically referred to as the "lump-sum death payment."

And there you have it. From double-deuce beer cans to lump-sum death payments, a short but informative tutorial on receiving death benefits if you too should suffer a similar tragedy and find yourself coping with the loss of your spouse.

Smile

It's such an easy thing, but it's tough to do. At least for me it is, after what happened. But I know it makes a difference. It helps other people out. It helps out my patients, my family, and my children. And that is what life is all about, trying to stay strong for myself and other people. I admit it does seem forced at times. Well, actually, a lot of the time. But

I do realize it's important. It's important to stay positive, to try to see a future. That's my one bit of advice if you're reading this and find yourself in a similar situation. Because the moment you stop smiling, you stop believing in a future, and that's the moment you give up. That's the worst thing you can do. Hopefully, at least for me, I won't have to force so many smiles. I am hopeful that day will come, and I am sure it will.

Sometimes

Sometimes I think this is all a dream, a really bad one. Sometimes I think that Catherine is still alive and one day I'll wake up and find her holding Declan or feeding Violet. But reality sets in every time I look in the mirror. I can see the truth in my eyes, and my reflection always blurs as my image becomes distorted with my own tears.

Sometimes I lie awake at night and think that I'll never sleep another minute, not another second for the rest of my life. This becomes ever so real as I turn and see the sunrise over the trees outside my window. But the next night I aways give in. I always lose, because exhaustion sets in. Exhaustion always wins, and it is a sweet victory.

Sometimes I hear my alarm in the morning and think, *Why even bother? Why get up today? What's the point? My wife's dead.* Then I think of my kids, my two children, and how they need me. In the end, I am all they have, and they are all I have. So I get out of bed. I start my new routine and go to work.

Sometimes I think I hear Catherine's voice when I'm at home. I quickly turn the corner, knowing all too well what I'll find. Emptiness. Nothingness.

Sometimes I hear a conversation or listen to a story and say in my head word for word what Catherine would have said in response. I always fight to hold back the tears because I know all too well that I'll never hear her speak any words again.

Sometimes I look at my children and wonder what I'll say to them when they're older. What will I tell them? What will I say about Catherine? I'll tell them how wonderful she was, how she loved them. But how can I make them understand? How can I make them realize what a special person their mother was? Sometimes I look at my children and cry because I know they will grow up without a mother.

Sometimes I hold my children, one at a time, while they cry and cry and cry. I hold them thinking that I can't do this for another second. I can't listen to them cry any longer. But I do; I always do. I hold them until they fall asleep, and they eventually always do.

Sometimes I feed Violet and hold my breath. I hold my breath until I think I can't hold it anymore because I'm scared. I'm terrified she'll spit up again, or worse. I'm scared she'll throw up her entire bottle. Sometimes she doesn't. Sometimes she does, and I worry about her. And I also think of Catherine, about how upset and scared and concerned she was when Violet would spit up or throw up her entire bottle. Yet I continue to feed Violet every time I can when I'm not at work.

Sometimes I see happy couples walking together, holding hands, living the dream, and I look back upon my life and feel empty. I feel lost, because I know that it's gone. My dream, my wife, my happiness—they're gone and can't be replaced.

Sometimes I struggle. Sometimes I feel lost. Sometimes I think I can't do this, I can't raise two children by myself, as a single father. I know I'm not in uncharted waters. I realize I'm not the only single father raising kids in America, raising two children born prematurely, two children who were sick, very sick, who spent almost three months in the hospital. A single father who lost his wife of almost eight years to suicide five months after their kids were born. I realize I'm not the only one in our society who now faces this challenge. I can't be, right?

Sometimes I wonder why my lips are dry. I know this sounds odd, but my lips have been cracked all winter long. And then I remember. Catherine. It always comes back to her. Catherine hated dry lips, and she always carried ChapStick with her, mostly for herself, but she always provided me some when she thought my lips were too dry. I then realize that this is my first winter without Catherine in over a decade, and my lips are living proof. I realize that this must sound ridiculous, even trivial to some, but that's the point. You don't comprehend how intertwined your life is with someone else's life until that person is gone. You set up a routine with your spouse, change it as necessary, and follow it, from paying bills to having children, making plans for the future, and even ChapStick. Now I have to start my own routine. I have to take care of myself because no one is around anymore to help me, let alone hand me ChapStick. So I stopped off at the drugstore on the way home from work today and bought some. I sat in my car in the parking lot and cried because as every day passes, it becomes more real. Catherine is not coming back, not now, not ever. I have to grow to understand this and live with it, but like a lot of other things in life, this is easier said than done.

Sometimes I close my eyes and see her face. I see her beautiful, smiling face looking at me. When I open my eyes, she's gone, and I know I will never see her again. I will never see her beautiful smile again.

Sometimes I wish it were Monday. And if it happens to be Monday, I actually want the following day to be another Monday. Sounds crazy, but it's true. I didn't use to be like this. I used to hate Mondays just like most everybody, just like most normal people. But now, things are different. Things have changed. I have changed. I have a hard time with the weekends now. It's when I miss Catherine the most. It's when I feel the most alone. I can be surrounded by friends, my in-laws, and, of course, my children, but I still feel alone. I still miss Catherine. The weekends afford me the down time to focus on my loss, my children's loss. During the week I'm busy at work. Say what you will about a job, about a career, but for me, it's a beautiful distraction. When I'm busy taking care of patients or doing procedures, I stay completely focused. I don't let my mind wander, I don't let myself think about what happened, think about my wife. And that's why I wish every day was Monday. Pretty sad, isn't it? Maybe one day I'll look forward to Fridays again, but I don't see that day coming anytime soon.

Sometimes I have meaningless, simple questions. Simple questions like "What should I get at the grocery store?" Sometimes I have more serious questions, like "Why did this happen?" or "Am I going to save enough money for my kids' college education?" And then I think I'll just talk to Catherine about it later when I get home. But now I can't. I can't talk to Catherine anymore. I can't talk to my wife, ever. I can't discuss what we should have for dinner. I can't talk to her about our kids—how to raise them, what to teach them. I can't do any of the things we had planned. Then I try to stop asking myself questions because I've come to realize that I will never have the answers, no matter how hard I try, no matter how long I think about them. Because some questions, the really difficult ones, are better left unanswered.

Sometimes I get very lonely while I drive. I've tried to get used to always being alone, especially when I drive, but it's still tough. No matter what I'm doing or where I'm going, I'm always alone. Either driving to work, running errands, or heading to the cemetery, I'm by myself. I occasionally look to my right while I drive and wish I could see Catherine sitting next to me. I wish I could look upon her smiling face and carry on just one more conversation. Instead, all I have keeping me company in my car is a half-empty Kleenex box sitting there, mocking me. When I realize that I'll never see my wife again, I usually grab another tissue to wipe my eyes and drive on ahead, alone with my thoughts and my box of Kleenex.

Sometimes I feel like I am treading water. I'm stuck in the middle of an ocean, flailing about, arms and legs constantly in motion, but I'm going nowhere, barely staying afloat. The problem with treading water is that I will eventually get tired. I will eventually run out of energy. I will eventually want to give up. I know that's not an option, but it's still a tempting proposition. I just hope I'll reach land one day. I hope my life stabilizes a little and I will no longer have to flail about, hopelessly lost. I don't think I can keep this up for too much longer.

Sometimes I think I should have done more, could have done more, to prevent this from happening. I lie awake at night wondering what I could have done differently. I revisit every day, every moment, every second I spent with Catherine after she was put on bed rest. People say that hindsight is twenty-twenty, and I can relate. But no matter how many times I replay the events of our lives together, especially the days leading up to her death, I can't tell you that I would have done anything differently. I live with the death of my wife, the death of the mother of our children, every day. I still struggle with it, and I realize that it will be a lifelong struggle. But when I look in the mirror, I tell myself that I did the best I could. I really did. Now the hard part is believing it.

Sometimes I think the sadness will never end, that the emptiness will always be there. As the days pass, I'm beginning to think that it always will be there, and that makes me sad. It sounds sort of ridiculous, but I get sad about the fact that I'm always sad. I've come to the point where I'm going to have to learn to live with it. I'm going to have to live my life, function in society, be the best father I can be, and learn to live with the sadness. As long as I can raise my kids and see them grow up healthy and happy, hopefully my sadness will eventually lessen. At least that's what I tell myself. Every morning I tell myself this, and it enables me to get out of bed. And sadly, that too is part of my new routine.

Spit Up

Have you ever tried to continually run uphill, without a break, nonstop? Probably not, but imagine it. You can be successful at first, but eventually you'll run out of steam. You'll fail. That's how I feel sometimes when I feed my daughter, Violet. It's been a constant struggle. Things have gotten a little better, but when we first brought her home from the hospital, it was difficult. It was a battle just to get her to drink from the bottle. And when she would finally eat, she would promptly refund most, if not all of her food on herself, on the floor, or, most often, on us. This went on every day, every four hours, for almost every feed. It was actually a little demoralizing because Catherine and I were so fixated on feeding our children the proper amount of calories as they were born so small, so prematurely. Catherine was also scared—no, terrified—that Violet wasn't growing, that she wasn't getting any bigger. She was obsessed with the fact that both of our kids were well below the tenth percentile on the growth chart. Catherine was never below the tenth percentile in any category, in anything, in her entire life. She had a problem handling the fact that our kids were so small, so tiny, for their actual age, and having Violet spit up her food, her calories, at almost every feed didn't help matters.

Yes, I quickly found out that a lot of babies spit up. I also learned that it's a really common problem for premature infants. But those facts didn't exactly ease Catherine's mind. She could care less about other babies; she just wanted our kids to grow and be healthy. We tried everything to help Violet out, from "heartburn" medicine and various combinations of different formulas to holding her upright and vertical for hours after every feed, which wasn't exactly easy. But nothing really worked except time. As days passed and she got older, she spit up a little less. Not much less when examined on a day-to-day basis, but over a span of several weeks she seemed to do a little better.

Unfortunately—well, really unfortunately—Catherine died well before Violet made any strides with her feeding. She's a lot better now. She still spits up from time to time, and she still occasionally loses her entire bottle on her shirt or on me. But she's getting there. She's improving. But with each advancement, with each milestone either one of our kids achieves, I still carry a heavy heart. I'm happy as I can be that our kids are getting better and are healthy, but it still tears me up that Catherine isn't alive to share these moments. It's hard to enjoy happiness by yourself. It's a lesson I have learned rather quickly over the past several weeks. I've had to teach myself to be happy for my kids and not focus on how sad I am that Catherine passed away. It's a lesson I haven't completely followed, but I'm trying. And that's what life is all about, trying to get better day by day. That's what I hope happens with my kids as well, that they get better and healthier every day.

Suicide

I can't pretend to understand suicide. I really can't. It's hard to comprehend something you would never do yourself. I now realize that Catherine suffered from postpartum depression. I understand that her illness led her to suicide, and it saddens me to no end. But the fact of the matter is, I will never truly understand it. Some people have told me that they would be angry or upset about what happened. Not me. I'm not mad at Catherine for what she did. I'm not angry at her. It actually fills me with sorrow to know that she was that upset, in that much pain.

Catherine and I shared everything, to a point. You can't possibly share every facet, every feeling you have with someone else. Catherine was no different. I knew she was upset. I knew she felt guilty at times. I told her it wasn't her fault, and I realize this probably fell on deaf ears. But I had no idea she was this upset, in this much pain.

I had no idea she was suffering from postpartum depression. It bothers me when I think of how upset she must have been, how much pain she had to have been in, to choose suicide as the only way out. This upsets me the most. I know how much she loved our kids. She really did. You don't spend eighteen hours a day, ninety-one days in a row, in the hospital with your kids without having total love for and devotion to them. I think that was almost the problem. She loved our kids so much and wanted so much for them, for them to do well and be healthy, that it upset her. And that pain translated to guilt, misplaced or not.

As far as I'm concerned, suicide will never be an option. I, unfortunately, right or wrong, am seeing a therapist. At the end of our first session, he asked me if I had suicidal thoughts. It was an expected question. Yet even though I knew it was coming, it still caught me by surprise. I remember telling him that it wasn't a concern. It wasn't a possibility for two reasons:

1. I could never leave my kids alone, with zero parents. Unacceptable.

2. I like myself too much. And I don't really care how that sounds to people, it's the truth.

Sunglasses

Catherine loved wearing sunglasses. She wore them all the time. If she would happen to accidentally forget them, which rarely happened, she would have to come back home just to pick up a pair. It could be completely gray outside, pouring down rain without a hint of sunshine on the horizon, and she would take her sunglasses, "just in case." The joke was that she had very sensitive eyes, and although I never really understood what that meant, she believed it.

It's a different story for me. I usually don't like to wear sunglasses. Don't get me wrong, if it's really sunny out, or if I'm driving and I need to see the road, trust me, I'm reaching for a pair of shades. But in general, I'd rather go without them.

The reason may sound a little absurd, but it's the truth. I like to look into people's eyes when I talk to them. I think you can learn a lot about somebody by just looking the person in the eyes when talking. Out of respect for the other person, I like to afford them the same possibility by not wearing my sunglasses all the time.

But now things are different. Whenever I talk to someone about Catherine passing away, I tend to look to the side, just far enough off angle where I'm not looking directly into their eyes as I discuss Catherine's death. Believe it or not, this happens quite often, sometimes twice a day, and it's been three months since she died. I see patients all the time, and most, if not all, of them know what has happened to me. So they ask me questions, lots of them. I don't begrudge them for asking, I really don't. I know they wouldn't ask if they didn't care. But it still hurts, it still brings to the surface a lot of pain. I'm not even exactly sure why I can't look people in the eyes when I talk about Catherine, but I just can't. I guess it's because I don't want people, specifically my patients, to see how much pain I'm in, how despondent I am. Plus, I want to avoid a complete meltdown in front of my patients. Personally, I feel that's pretty bad form, and, fortunately, I've avoided that situation so far. I haven't doubled over in tears in front of any of my patients yet, but I've come pretty damn close. I think the only way I've avoided it so far is that I always look off to the side and avoid eye contact when I talk about what has happened to me.

I hope one day it'll change. I want to come to work and not be worried about the questions, about what people, what my patients, will ask me. I hope that if they do inquire, I can look them in the eyes and talk about it without fear of losing it in front of them. I've actually thought about bringing sunglasses to work, just in case. But I've decided that is probably not a good look for a physician. So for the time being, I'm going to do the best I can. One day, maybe, I can revert back to my old ways. Maybe I will start looking people in the eyes without fear.

Tears

This is one thing I haven't been short of lately, and it's definitely a new addition to my routine. I was never one to cry in the past. I'm not saying that because I'm macho or anything; it's just a fact. It's probably because of two factors. On the surface, the most glaring thing is that I am a guy, and in our society it's really not an acceptable thing for men to sit around and shed tears all day. But I think the real reason is that I just haven't experienced any real tragedies or despair prior to 2012 to cause me to be so upset I would end up crying.

Prior to my wife passing away, I can recall three separate occasions in the past twenty-five years when I cried. And two out of those three times were within the previous five months. About two and a half decades ago, I cried when my grandfather died. I have very little recollection of this, but I do recall him passing away suddenly and unexpectedly in his sleep. I don't know for certain the real cause of his death, but the most likely explanation is that he had a heart attack.

I do remember how much I loved my grandpa. I can recall fondly my mom bringing my brother and me over to our grandparents' house when we were young. I thought the world of him, and when he died a small part of my childhood died with him. It was my first real experience with death, with any kind of loss, really. I remember grieving his death even at that young age.

The other two times I cried involved my children. Declan was born first, almost five hours before Violet, and I cried when he came into this world. He was so small and so helpless, and there was nothing I could do for him. There was a whole team of doctors and nurses waiting for him, and they whisked him away in seconds to take care of him. I remember looking up at Catherine and she looked so scared, so tired, and so beautiful, and I couldn't help myself. I put her hand in mine and we cried together.

Fast-forward thirty days. Thirty days of darkness, thirty days of pain, thirty days of fear. We had been basically living at the hospital, Catherine more than me because I had gone back to work. But I was there in the evenings with her to share the pain. Both of our kids were still very sick, Declan much more so than Violet. My son needed heart surgery to repair a defect in order for him to live. He had actually gone through the surgery without any complications, but afterward it was a different story. What followed was the longest night of my life; well, at least it was until Catherine died. The doctors had to bring in a special ventilator to help him breathe and exchange oxygen because he was literally not breathing at all. Being in the medical profession, I knew how sick he really was, and I was so scared. Catherine, understandably, was a complete mess. She was all tears, all the time, and I tried to remain strong. I tried to be the glue for our family and show confidence, be supportive, and be the strong husband. I stayed up all night with Catherine, holding her, telling her everything was going to be all right, although I was really just making that up at the time. I had no idea if Declan was going to live to take another breath, let alone see the sunrise the following morning. I stayed with Catherine while she wept. I stayed with her until she cried herself to sleep.

It must have been five the following morning when I left the hospital room. Declan was still fighting, and was slowly improving by that time. Catherine was asleep. I stole away for some privacy, to clear my head, even though I knew that was an impossibility. There was a small, private room right off the NICU for parents, and that's were I went. I slowly peeked inside, saw nobody was there, and dove in. I basically collapsed onto a couch in that small room and completely lost it. I cried uncontrollably. I even scared myself; I never knew I could weep like that. I was glad I had gotten away because I didn't want to wake Catherine up, and I also didn't want her to see me like this, totally helpless, lost in despair. I'd never thought I could ever feel pain like that. I wouldn't wish that pain on anybody, for any reason—pure, raw despair—and I let it out that morning. The unfortunate thing is, that pain would be all too familiar, all too consuming, just four months later when Catherine hung herself.

I am a different person now after what I've been through. How could I not be? My kids were in the hospital for three months, my son almost died after heart surgery, and now my wife has passed away. Tears are second nature now; they are a part of my new routine. I'm not saying I walk around like a bumbling idiot, crying all over the place, scaring people. No, it's not like that, but close. I spend the day trying to distract myself, attempting to separate myself from my own feelings of emptiness. Fortunately, work offers somewhat of a distraction, which is helpful. I expend a tremendous amount of energy keeping my emotions at bay, just under the surface, like a wild animal in captivity trying to escape. Even the sixty seconds of silence of a walk down a hospital hallway can sometimes be enough time for my emotions, my tears, to surface. But thankfully, or luckily, I've been able to tame my emotions, for the most part. I keep them tucked away in silence, in captivity. I tend to save them for the car. My tears come out on my commute home. They tend to show themselves in full force when I'm in my car alone, which is understandable, since my tears have been held in check all day while I'm at work.

It's even painful when I drive between the office and the hospital, which is only a fifteen-minute commute. I can't explain how difficult it is to carry on your work day after you've been sitting in your car grieving for your dead wife. I often stay in my car in the hospital parking lot for several minutes trying to compose myself before going in to see patients. I know for certain that my patients don't want to look up and see my sad, tearful eyes offering medical advice. Somehow, I do my best and carry on. I stay professional and bury my emotions when I visit my patients. Like I said, the distraction of work is helpful.

That hour-long commute home is also brutal, with nothing but my thoughts and memories to keep me company, but it also affords me the time to continue to grieve. I spend the drive, that alone time, trying to process things that will never make sense. I remember Catherine, her love for our children, and I cry. It's painful, especially for someone who has been so unaccustomed to crying, but I admit, for some reason, it helps. It's been seventy days since she passed away as I write this, and things really haven't gotten much better. I'm hopeful for the day I can drive home in peace and not weep for the loss of my wife, when I can fill my mind with thoughts of hope, of the future, and not cry for my children who will never know their mother.

Text Message
3:15 p.m.
September 24, 2012

That's when she sent me a text message. Just three days before she died, Catherine texted me a picture of Declan with a wide-eyed, ear-to-ear smile with the following message: "Cheesin'. Trying to elicit a grin from Ms. V."

I responded with my own grin and text message: "Cheesin'...I love it!!!"

Seventy-two hours later, my wife was gone.

The Lonely Claw

It's funny how certain things can trigger emotions, trigger memories out of nowhere. I was following my new weekend routine and actually having a decent morning. Well, as decent as can be considering the circumstances. I had just finished feeding the kids, and for once everything went pretty smoothly. Limited crying, no fussing, and they both drank their bottles without incident. Even better, they both promptly passed out and went right to sleep afterward. I headed to the kitchen with plans to drink some coffee in peace. It seemed like it was turning out to be a good day until I looked down and found a tiny, lonely claw lying on the floor.

And then it hit me, like a Mack truck screaming down a highway. As I stopped in my tracks to bend over to pick it up, I was overcome with emotions. Sadly, this innocent cat's claw reminded me of the past, the past I used to love but can no longer have anymore.

A few weeks after the twins were discharged from the hospital, I had come home from work and Catherine was at her usual place, sitting in the living room with our kids. She had a big smile on her face, and I knew something was up, because she was not exactly full of smiles those days. She said, "Come over here," and when I approached her, she dropped this very tiny object in my hand. Before I could even ask what it was, I looked down and saw a little cat's claw. She then said, "Who do think it belongs to?" She was referring to our two cats, Olive and Cleo. I replied with a smile, "Not sure, but I can do some investigating." It went on from there, turning into our own private joke. You know, the moments and times you share with your spouse, the inside joke that nobody understands but still amuses you and your best friend. From then on, when I would come home from work, she would often ask me if I figured out which one of our cats had "lost a claw."

I readily admit, just writing this down seems incredibly ridiculous, but it was something I shared with Catherine. When I saw that tiny, lonely claw that day, I thought of Catherine. I thought of what I would say to her if she were still alive. I would tell her, "I found another claw! Let's find out who it belongs to."

But I couldn't, and never will be able to. And that's why I cried. Instead of drinking coffee in my kitchen and enjoying a quiet, peaceful morning, I sat down on the floor and cried, alone in my thoughts. I felt like a fool, sitting on the floor in my house, holding a cat's claw, crying. But that's what I did. You find yourself doing strange things when your wife kills herself and you have newborn twins who were sick, who were born three months early. You find yourself sitting on the floor, crying by yourself, holding a cat's claw in your hand. Unfortunately, it appears that those strange things become part of your new routine, which is also sad.

Time for Yourself

There is no secret to surviving the loss of your spouse. There's no specific therapy you can follow, there's no particular medical regimen that will alleviate your pain or cure your sadness. Trust me, I wish there was, because I would try it. But there is one recommendation I can offer that I have found helpful, although it's not always that easy to accomplish. But it's still something you should try if you are unfortunate enough to find yourself in a similar tragic situation. I would recommend finding time for yourself. Time, a limitless commodity. It's a simple recommendation, but a powerful one nonetheless. You need to find time to work through things, to process your emotions, time to allow yourself to grieve, to heal. At least that's what I've found to be useful.

Fortunately, I have a lengthy commute to work every day, which I use to my advantage. It doesn't sound like much, but between work, taking care of my kids, and life in general, that drive to and from work is priceless. I use that time to think about my past. I try to focus on the good times, which was my entire life spent with Catherine before she passed away. Despite what has happened with my kids and their health, I still look back upon my life with Catherine and miss it. I miss everything about it. Mostly, I just miss her. I also use this time to think about my life now and how I became a widower. I realize it's pointless to try to figure out why this happened, but I still think about it. It's human nature, I guess. But no matter how hard I think about it, how many times I review the events that transpired that day or that preceding week, I come up blank. I have no answers. I also think about the future, my kids' future. Although I have no plans, and sometimes I feel like I have no idea what I'm doing, I can only hope things will get better, because it seems they can't get any worse.

I do all this thinking while I drive. I believe it's helpful, to a point. I certainly can't grieve and deal with my loss at work. I also don't have time to worry about my emptiness, my sadness, when I'm at home feeding my kids or changing their diapers. So I've cut out a little time every day for myself. Although it's not much, it'll have to do. At this point in my life, I'll take it.

Time of Death

Time. It's really sort of irrelevant. You can try to control it, you can try to track it, but you can't. It keeps marching on, with no regard for you or anybody else. You can also try to pinpoint certain moments. You can try to bookmark a particular incident, a certain event in your life. But in the end, it doesn't matter. It really doesn't matter what time something happened. It's the actual event that's important. This is a lesson I have taught myself over the past one hundred eleven days, something I have come to terms with.

After Catherine died, I became fixated on her time of death. Not that it mattered in the scheme of things, because she obviously decided to do it while I was away at work. But I wanted to know because of our kids; I wanted to know how long they were left alone. I know Catherine cared about them. I know she loved our kids and she wouldn't have done this if she wasn't in pain, if she wasn't sick. But I still wanted to know when she did it, when she left our kids alone. I went so far as to call the coroner and ask for the time of death. I was completely expecting an educated medical estimate, maybe a one- to two-hour window. You watch *CSI* on TV and they can pinpoint time of death with ridiculous accuracy. They use body temperature, insects, shadows, and a paper clip and can tell you within the minute when someone died. But it's not the same in real life. It's nowhere near the same in reality. The coroner couldn't even tell me with any sort of confidence when Catherine died. I was lucky to hear them commit to the fact that she died on September 27, 2012, let alone any particular time that day. I remember telling the coroner on the phone that she was alive when I left for work at six that morning and my mother-in-law called me at 4:19 p.m. after she found Catherine in my closet. But that didn't help the situation. The coroner had no idea when she killed herself.

After I hung up the phone, I put it out of my mind, because in the end, it really doesn't matter. There are two indisputable facts about the case. Catherine loved our kids unconditionally. And she was sick and in pain and killed herself. In the end, the time of her death is irrelevant. That's one of the hardest things I have come to terms with.

Tired of Being Alone

During the summer of 1999, my routine involved a steady dose of Al Green. For multiple reasons, it was a long summer for me. I was working nights waiting tables at a restaurant, and all of my roommates had day jobs, so I would get up every day and basically be by myself until I left for work at around five. Trust me, I'm not the kind of guy who requires constant company, and even back then I enjoyed the time alone. However, like anything in life, the alone time eventually wore on me. Plus, I was getting over my previous girlfriend and overall was in kind of a funk. I knew Catherine by then. We had actually met four years earlier in 1995 during our freshman year in college. However, we were not technically dating at this time. It's funny how time and perspective changes you. In the summer of 1999, I was twenty-two years old, and I thought getting over my ex-girlfriend was the end of the world. Now fast-forward to 2012. I am in my midthirties, father of twin newborns who spent several months in the hospital, and my wife of almost eight years had recently hung herself in our bedroom closet.

Well, I digress. My routine that summer was to sleep in, catch up on the sports scores by watching *SportsCenter* on ESPN, then head out to our front porch and listen to Al Green on our stereo. I would let the CD play through maybe once before I would set it to repeat on "Tired of Being Alone." I would drink coffee and read Stephen King books for hours every afternoon while listening to Al Green.

It was on one particular summer day while listening to my guy on the stereo that I looked up and saw Catherine on the sidewalk. She wore a white summer dress, and she looked absolutely stunning. I was also a little confused how she had gotten to my house because I hadn't seen her car drive by. Back then, she cruised around in this little white Jeep Wrangler, and I hadn't seen it pull up. Plus, since we weren't dating at that time, it was a little unclear why she was even there.

She must have seen the surprise on my face as she walked up the porch steps. She cracked a little smile—actually, a beautiful little smile—and asked how I was. I immediately responded, "How did you get here?"

Her smile grew ever so slightly, and she said she'd walked. At the time, I couldn't believe it. She never walked *anywhere* for *anybody*! It's not like she was out of shape or not athletic. She was actually quite thin, but she was not a person who ever just took walks. It's not like her apartment was on the other side of the city—it was probably about a forty-minute walk—but it was definitely out of character for her. She was the type of person who would aggressively hunt around the parking lot to find the closest possible space just to prove a point—and to not have to walk any further than needed.

That's when I knew. Looking back at that moment, I knew she was the one. I remember that moment like it was yesterday. We sat and talked for hours, sitting in the sun on my porch, listening to music. She joked and gave me a hard time about Al Green. Later on, I drove her home before I went to work. You know, to save her a walk. After that day everything changed. We went out, dated, and eventually married.

That leads me to the present. Almost full circle, if you will. I am a little older, considerably wiser, and have a hell of a lot more responsibility, including two children. I know I will never truly be alone. I am closer with my brother now, and I have built a strong bond with my in-laws having gone through this tragedy together. But the fact remains that, deep down, I feel very alone. The unfortunate truth is, there's a very strong possibility that that will never change. And that saddens me, the black-and-white reality of my life.

I do my best to keep my head up, go to work every day, and come home and take care of my kids. Press repeat, and that's my new routine. But there are many days I feel like I don't have the energy to get out of bed. It's like I'm too tired. I'm tired of many things these days. Especially, I'm "Tired of Being Alone."

These Eyes

These eyes cry every night for you
These arms long to hold you again

The hurtin's on me, yeah
And I will never be free

These eyes watched you bring my world to an end
This heart could not accept and pretend

These eyes are cryin'
These eyes have seen a lot of loves
But they're never gonna see another one like I had with you
(Guess Who)

Tragedy

The true definition of tragedy varies. It's dependent on each individual's frame of reference. And it mostly depends on how closely you personally are affected by the specific tragedy. From afar, tragedy can be sad. It's just human nature to feel compassion and be upset over the loss and consequences of real tragedy, no matter if it happened across the street or it occurred on the other side of the country. But it's a completely different story when tragedy becomes personal, when you become the center of the story.

That's where I come in. That's my story, a story I had to eventually share with my therapist. It's one thing to write in down on paper or type it out on a laptop, but it's a completely different experience to share your tragedy in blow-by-blow detail with someone else, in person. But that's what I had to do at my first therapy session. It wasn't easy, by any means. Just making the appointment and walking in the door was one of the toughest things I found myself doing in a long time. Just admitting that I needed help was a gut check. Admitting that I couldn't handle the situation, admitting that I needed some assistance, was a truly eye-opening experience, one that I wanted to avoid at all costs. But in the end, I realized that nobody is perfect. I learned that it's OK to ask for help sometimes.

So I went to therapy once a week, for several weeks. But no medications, no prescription or nonprescription drugs—right or wrong, I refused any pharmacologic assistance. I needed to keep my head clear, and that's been a personal choice I've always held and will never change. All in all, I think the first therapy session was the most helpful. It allowed me to actually get a few hours of sleep at night. It helped resolve some issues I had with guilt. Don't get me wrong, therapy is not an antidote, it's not a quick fix. It's more like a Band-Aid for a slowly oozing wound. It helps right the ship but doesn't steer the boat. But that's all you can really ask for, isn't it, a little guidance along the way?

At the end of our first therapy session I could quantify the nature of my personal tragedy. I was at least able to subjectively measure it from a professional's viewpoint. As I gathered my things and got up to leave, I turned and asked my therapist one final question. I asked him what he thought of my experiences. I asked him what he thought about everything I've been through, from my twins being born prematurely and spending months in the hospital to seeing my son almost die after heart surgery and becoming a widower just six weeks shy of our eighth wedding anniversary. What followed I will never forget. My therapist—who, I might add, is quite experienced, probably in his early seventies, and been around the block a few times—turned to me and calmly replied, "This is probably one of the worst tragedies that I can remember."

Those words have stuck with me. They're ingrained in my mind, not because of their significance but because I'm still going. I still get up every day. I still go to work, and I still come home. I still take care of my kids every day. Because I haven't given up. Not that that was ever a choice. It was never an option. I firmly believe that tragedies should not define you; you should be defined by how you respond to tragedy. And that's how I will live my life from here on out. Because despite what happens to you in life, no matter what cards you're dealt, you have to play your hand. It's up to you how you play it. That's your choice. And in the game of life, I plan on winning.

Unforgettable

Unforgettable, that's what you are
Unforgettable, though near or far
Like a song of love that clings to me
How the thought of you does things to me

Never before has someone been more

Unforgettable, in every way
And forevermore, that's how you'll stay
(And forevermore, that's how you'll stay)
(Natalie Cole)

Vitamins

Vitamins were a struggle, a constant source of aggravation, a daily reminder that our kids weren't healthy, that they were premature, that they needed extra help, extra medications. At least that's how it was in the beginning. It's not normal to give your baby a dark, slimy, foul-smelling substance on a daily basis. But that's what we did, once a day, every day. And I still do. It was worse back then, and Catherine hated it. She absolutely did, and so did I. We mixed the vitamins with the formula once a day, at least we did for Declan. Violet, well, she wouldn't have any of that. When she was still in the hospital and we tried to mix her vitamins with her formula, she would promptly turn her head and refund the entire bottle, that was if she would even drink any of her food in the first place. She would usually just refuse to eat if her formula was mixed with the vitamins. It's funny to think babies have taste buds and preferences at that young age, but they do. At least Violet did. And I didn't blame her; those vitamins smelled terrible. So we ended up drawing up her vitamins in a tiny syringe and feeding them directly into her mouth, which was successful, to a point. She usually spit most of it back up, and she would end up covered in that dark, slimy substance. It was almost comical. It would have been funny if we hadn't had to repeat that same ritual, that same routine, every day.

I kept up the routine as long as I could after Catherine died. But after a few weeks, I couldn't take it anymore. I decided to try to mix her vitamins with her formula, just as we'd done for Declan for the past six months. Fortunately, at least for my sanity, it worked. Since Violet was finally drinking a larger quantity of formula during her feedings, the vitamins were diluted enough that she actually tolerated them. She would finally drink her bottle and not promptly throw up her entire feeding. It was a minor success, a small stepping-stone on the path to sanity that first day I tried this little experiment. I remember being ecstatic, almost delirious with happiness, that I no longer had to shoot a syringeful of blackness into my daughter's mouth. At the same time, I was also sad I couldn't share that success with her mother, with my wife, with Catherine. I finally realized that's how our lives will be from now on. That's how our new routine will be. No matter what happens, no matter how things go, my kids have only me to depend on. I know I am the sole provider and parent for my kids. So for every disappointment, every minor success, and every major milestone, I have to accept and live with it by myself. And that's my new life, that's my new routine.

Wanting More for My Kids

I never really envisioned what life would be like with kids. I just expected Catherine and I would figure things out as we went along. I'm almost positive my wife had some semblance of a plan, mostly because she always did. But things went sideways quickly after she gave birth three months early. At that point, all I really wanted was for my kids to make it home safely from the hospital, which they eventually did.

But now things are different. Very different. I do start to think about the future, about what to do and how to take care of my kids. I now realize that I am a single parent, which is not entirely strange in today's society. But being a single father is a little more rare. According to the Population Reference Bureau, approximately 5 percent of children grow up in a single father household, compared to about 24 percent of children who grow up in a single mother household. That leads me to where I am now, thinking about raising my kids and how I am going to accomplish this. Fortunately, I'm not alone. I have the love and support of my in-laws and friends, but it's not the same.

And now I can't really give my kids more than what I had as a child growing up. That's sort of what life is all about anyway. Doing more, providing more for your children than what you actually had when you were a child. It sounds simple, but it's really a powerful goal. It's a way that as society we can continually better ourselves. Financially, I can provide more for my kids than what I had. I was never poor growing up, but I was never privileged. I had a typical, suburban, lower-middle-class upbringing, and that was fine by me. I know that I can offer my children more options. Private school, music lessons, foreign language classes, college tuition, and on and on if I so choose. Not that all those things are crucial to a happy childhood and life, but it's still nice to be able to provide those things for your children.

But when it comes right down to it, I won't be able to offer the basics, and that is two loving parents. That is what kills me. It really does eat at me at times because that was supposed to be the easy part, at least for Catherine and me. It was never even an option that another outcome was a possibility. It was just understood. We would be together forever and raise our children and make decisions together. We would stumble together, get up together, and survive together—one big happy family. Now I can't provide this. And that's the reality of the situation.

Weekend Out

It was a beautiful weekend, not because it was the last weekend I ever spent with my wife, which in all honesty is a good enough reason. It was because we were happy. At least, I was happy. I thought she was too.

The last weekend Catherine was alive, her parents did us a huge favor. They took the kids that weekend. They packed the little ones up and took them to their house on Saturday morning. It seemed like a small miracle, an abbreviated holiday. For the first time in months, Catherine and I finally had time for each other. She was happy that weekend, I promise you that. She may have been battling demons at times, and she probably was, but for that weekend, we both had a momentary escape from reality. We even went out to dinner Saturday night. We hadn't eaten out in an actual restaurant in almost six months. It was almost an out-of-body experience, going out on a date like any other regular couple. We weren't visiting the hospital, changing diapers, holding crying kids, or doing laundry. We were actually out in the world, living. I still remember what we talked about. I remember what she wore. I remember everything about that night. And I also remember that we were in love.

My memories of Catherine are a double-edged sword. I cherish the good times, which were plentiful. You don't know someone for half your life or live with someone for over ten years without being happy, at least that's my opinion. And it's true, because we were happy, and there are plenty of reasons why. But I also remember the pain. I remember how sick our kids were. I recall how we both went to the hospital every day for months. And I remember how Catherine changed, how upset she was at times, how she silently blamed herself for what happened to our kids. These memories haunt me, they slowly tear at my soul. I try to fight off these memories, but sometimes I can't help myself. But I know I can't go on, I can't live my life, if I don't focus on what we had together, if I don't appreciate how wonderful Catherine was. So that's what I try to do. That's how I choose to move on. It's not easy, but nobody said life was going to be. I hold onto the good times like a life preserver, so I can stay afloat while I live my life. I hold onto the days when we were happy, like that last weekend we went out to dinner, that last weekend she was alive.

White Pumpkin

Catherine died about a month before Halloween. Befitting the season, her best friend placed a small, white pumpkin at her gravesite. I have to admit, it was actually a tasteful addition. I know Catherine would have appreciated the gesture.

As the days passed, as the days rolled on, that white pumpkin stayed there at her gravesite. Although no ever took it and no one ever moved it, it slowly began to change. It gradually began to get smaller. Her gravesite was surrounded by nothing but grass, countless trees, and, yes, squirrels. That white pumpkin was too tempting, too appetizing, to be left alone. As the days passed, the pumpkin was slowly devoured, slowly eaten by the wildlife, by the squirrels. It was actually kind of humorous, if one can find humor when surrounded by death, when in a cemetery. Every time I would come back to visit, that pumpkin would be a little smaller, a little more chewed up. I know even Catherine would have found it amusing. As the weeks rolled by and fall turned into winter, that pumpkin was eventually devoured and snow covered the gravesite. I think I'll get another small, white pumpkin next fall. I think Catherine would appreciate it, I really do. If nothing else, I'm pretty sure the squirrels will be thankful, as I know they'll enjoy it.

Witching Hour

The witching hour is another name for newborn babies' evening fussiness, or what I refer to as absolute lunacy. Whoever coined the phrase obviously never had kids, because it's really misrepresenting the truth to limit the witching hour to just sixty minutes. To be more precise, to be just a tad more accurate, the phrase should be revised to "witching hours," because when my kids get worked up, they can really go. Seriously, both of my kids can scream, cry, and holler for what seems like an eternity. It's bad enough when one of them gets upset and loses it, but it's downright insanity when they're both wailing away at the same time.

For obvious reasons, it was much more tolerable when Catherine was alive. I would hold one baby, and she would hold the other. If that didn't work, we would switch off. Trust me, it wasn't easy, and we were exhausted, but at least we had each other. Now it's all different. Everything has changed. I'm lucky that I'm not alone, that I have help and my in-laws basically stay with me. But it's not the same, not just for the obvious reason that Catherine has passed away. It goes deeper than that, and it saddens me. For some reason, and I know this doesn't make sense, sometimes I think they are crying for their mom. Sometimes I think they miss Catherine. I completely understand that my kids are a little over seven months old, and to be developmentally accurate, they are only four months old when you correct for the expected due date. So in reality, it's almost absurd to think that they cry because Catherine isn't here anymore. Nonetheless, I still believe that subconsciously both of my kids know. They know she isn't around anymore. They both saw Catherine every day for one hundred forty consecutive days before she died. She visited them in the hospital, held them, fed them, changed their diapers, and played with them for one hundred forty consecutive days. So I choose to believe they miss their mom, their mother. And that hurts, it pains me.

That's why the witching hour(s) can be the most disheartening, the saddest. Thankfully, as my kids have gotten older, the crying, their fussiness, has gradually decreased. But when it still happens, I tend to cry right along with them. Not all the time on the outside, but I do on the inside. I try to tell myself everything will be OK, at least that's what I whisper in their ears when I try to console them. I just hope that this time around I'm telling the truth and not lying to myself. I hope everything will be OK, and I hope one day I can say those words and finally believe them.

Without You

Can't live if living is without you
I can't live, I can't give anymore
I can't live if living is without you

Can't live, I can't give anymore
(Living is without you)
(Harry Nilsson)

Writing

I never intended to write a book. But I also never planned on being widowed in my midthirties, so you never really know what life has in store for you. Before this, I hadn't written anything since those school assignments everybody had to do when we were kids. I only started writing as a way to process my thoughts, my emotions, and, most importantly, my pain. I used writing as therapy, as a way to heal, just like patients use medicine when they get sick. And just like any real illness, such as an incurable cancer or a massive heart attack, medicine or therapy can help the healing process. But you are never the same. After any significant tragedy or medical illness, you may eventually improve, you may eventually be able to cope with life again, but you are never truly the same.

I tried to write as often as I could, which clearly was not often enough. I would write between patients in the office, late at night because I couldn't sleep, while sitting in my car in the hospital parking lot, or after the kids were finally quiet and asleep. I actually wrote over 90 percent of this book in my head as I drove back and forth to work every day. My mind would always race, nonstop, as I commuted every morning and every evening. I would try to remember my thoughts and jot them down the next time I had a moment of free time.

I also never thought about what I would do with this book until I was about halfway done. In the days and weeks since Catherine died, I heard countless stories, most of them from strangers, about how he or she knew somebody or was related to someone who suffered from depression or postpartum depression or who had committed suicide. I began to realize how pervasive this problem is, this illness. I thought that if this book could help even one person, one family, survive this tragedy or, better yet, avoid this tragedy, than it would be a success. Even if it doesn't, even if no one ever reads this book, I can tell you that it helped at least one person. It helped one person cope, it helped one person survive, it helped one person live. And that's me. When it's all said and done, I need to pick up the pieces and live so I can take care of my kids.

Xmas

You're going to have to cut me a little slack on this one. There are not too many words in the English language that start with the letter X, so I picked Xmas. It was really the only option.

It was the toughest holiday by far. Every day is hard, but for the obvious reasons, Christmas was rough. I guess I could have chosen to not even celebrate the holidays. I could have just skipped it. I don't think anybody would have blamed me, considering the circumstances. Even if someone had had a problem with it, I'm sure no one would have said anything. One could even argue that the kids wouldn't even know the difference, since they were so young. But I don't believe that. And even though deep down that may be true, it still doesn't make it right. I had to go through with the holidays because even though I had lost my wife, I still had to live.

So when the time came, I dug out the old fake tree from the basement and hauled out the ornaments and decorations from the back closet. I put on Pandora radio, flicked to the holiday station, and pushed play. I spent the afternoon doing what I would have normally done with Catherine but with her mom and sister instead. I started a new routine. I put up the tree and lights, followed by the stockings, one for Declan and one for Violet, and I finished with all the decorations.

The hardest part was when I came across a white gumdrop wreath that Catherine had made two years ago. I remembered how long she had worked on that wreath, how many hours she had spent making it. I also remember how disappointed she was when she had finally finished. I thought it was nice, but it didn't turn out exactly how she had envisioned it. Yet I hung it up on the wall, just as we had the previous two years. The other difficult time was when I fished out an ornament we had received on our wedding day, eight years ago. It was a pretty silver ornament with our wedding date inscribed on the top. I remember holding the ornament in my hand, tears welling up in my eyes, unsure of what I should do. My first instinct was to not hang it up, that it would be too tough to see. But after some thought, and a few tears, I decided to go ahead and put it on the tree. For some reason I wanted it up there; I wanted to see our wedding ornament on our tree.

The days rolled on. I showed the tree to my kids several times, holding them up in front of it. They were still very young, but I believe they enjoyed looking at the lights. When Christmas finally arrived, I pushed right on ahead. Trust me, I didn't really want to. I felt like hiding away in my bed, but I knew I had to press on. I actually had to round at the hospital Christmas morning, and going to work did provide a little escape, a small distraction. When I came home, we opened presents with my in-laws. The kids seemed to enjoy holding the wrapping paper more than looking at their new toys or clothes, but they seemed happy nonetheless. Although everybody seemed to enjoy the day, everybody seemed to be smiling, there was still a deep sadness in the air, a sadness that holiday music, bright lights, or presents couldn't overcome.

I just hope that as my children get older the holidays become a little easier. I know that they probably won't. I know that the sadness will always be there, hiding in the background, waiting to dispense my tears.

But I still have hope. And when you feel that you don't have anything else to hold onto, you have to hold onto hope.

Yarn

About two months into Catherine's pregnancy, she taught herself how to knit. She picked up a how-to book, bought some yarn—organic, of course—and set to work. Her initial projects were small yet satisfying. She knitted a few scarves and then made two small winter hats for the twins. After we found out that my brother's wife was also pregnant, she started knitting a blanket for their child. Catherine's project was briefly sidetracked after she was admitted to the hospital for bed rest, but after she gave birth, she picked it back up. Looking back, I think she knitted while our kids were in the NICU to give her something to do. Early on, when both of our kids were in their incubators, there was nothing we could do but sit with them in their hospital room. We couldn't really hold them, and we certainly couldn't bottle-feed them, so I think Catherine knitted just to keep herself busy. I can't tell you how many countless days I would come to the hospital after work and find her sitting in the twins' hospital room, knitting silently, always keeping one eye on them. Even though there was nothing we could do for them, she would always keep a watchful eye on them, hoping they would get better, wishing they would get bigger, stronger, healthier.

Toward the end of their NICU stay, she finally finished the blanket. It was a large, very soft, cream-colored blanket, and it was beautiful. She mailed it out to my brother the next day and started on a new blanket for Declan. That's when our kids were transferred to the step-down unit. They were slowly getter stronger, and they both no longer needed incubators and were in their own cribs. They were still impossibly small, but they at least started to look a little healthier. That's when everything started to become more real, parenting, that is. Even though we were still trapped in the false environment of the hospital, we were now able to hold our kids. We were also able to dress them in very tiny preemie clothing. We started to bottle-feed them and even give them baths. They also started crying more, a lot more. Because we were more active, more hands-on with our kids, Catherine didn't really have time to work on her new blanket anymore. She actually never finished it. I still have the half-knitted blanket at home, under my coffee table. I have no idea what I'll do with it. I certainly can't knit, so I have no intention of finishing it. But I also don't have the heart to get rid of it. It's hard to explain, but I hope one day it does get finished. I just don't know how that will ever happen.

My brother gave me back that cream-colored organic blanket Catherine made. It took me by surprise because I had actually forgotten about it. He gave it back a few days after Catherine died when he came to visit and help me grieve the loss of my wife. I have that blanket on my chair in my bedroom, folded up. I hope to one day give it to my kids when they are a little bit older, a little more mature. I want to tell them that their mother made that blanket, that she'd taught herself how to knit. I want to tell them what a wonderful person, what a truly loving mother, she was. I want to do all those things one day, yet I almost dread it at the same time, having to explain to my children what happened, answering their questions, talking about their mother. But I will, I want to, and I owe it to Catherine to do so. I know it will be hard, just like anything else in life. Nothing comes easy, and I'm all too familiar with that concept.

Yesterday

Yesterday
All my troubles seemed so far away
Now it looks as though they're here to stay
Oh, I believe in yesterday

Suddenly,
I'm not half the man I used to be

There's a shadow hanging over me
Oh, yesterday came suddenly

Why she
Had to go I don't know, she wouldn't say
I said
Something wrong, now I long for yesterday

Yesterday
Love was such an easy game to play
Now I need a place to hide away
Oh, I believe in yesterday
(Beatles)

"Zou Bisou Bisou"

Catherine loved the show *Mad Men*. It was one of the few shows we recorded. It's not like we watched a lot of television anyway, mostly HGTV or Food Network programs, sparingly few prime time shows, football, and *Mad Men*. We watched even less television after she went on bed rest this past spring. In fact, these days, I can barely watch TV anymore. I don't even try, really. I have it on in the background sometimes, and my in-laws will watch TV occasionally, but I can't. I have trouble focusing now. At this point, I can really only concentrate on two things:

1. Taking care of my kids.

2. Taking care of my patients.

That's it. Otherwise, I just can't seem to focus anymore, certainly not on television shows. I even have a hard time watching sports, which was my one and only hobby before all this happened. I sit down to watch a football game and five minutes later I find myself getting up and moving on—to play with the kids, check on the laundry, scoop the cat litter, something, anything. I just need to keep myself busy, keep myself distracted. In fact, I can't even remember the last television show I watched all the way to the end.

But I do recall the show *Mad Men* and how much Catherine loved the series. Toward the end of the show's last season, one of the main characters, Jessica Pare, sang a song, "Zou Bisou Bisou." Every now and then, I hear this same song on the radio. Not often, but often enough. Every time I hear it, I think of Catherine. I think back to the days before she went on bed rest, before the world became dark and gray, when she was happy, when she was whole. And I smile. We had so many great times together, so many years of happiness. Sometimes these memories get lost; they seem buried at times beneath layers of sadness and pain. But I try to hold onto the good memories. I need to hold onto them, not just for myself but for our kids. I have a responsibility to pass on Catherine's kindness, her warmth, her very being to our children. And I intend to, no matter how hard it is to get back to that point, to get back that time in my life when we were both whole. If it takes a silly song from some television show, so be it. Whatever it takes, I'll use it, because Catherine was a wonderful, incredible human being. When my children get older, I'll tell them about her. Although I know it'll be difficult, it'll be painful, I actually look forward to sharing her life with them, because they need to know about their mother. Right or wrong, they need to know.

Conclusion

Sometimes I feel lucky. Not often, mind you, but occasionally I do. I realize that must seem oddly placed, especially after reading about the pain and sorrow that have literally consumed my life. But you cannot get to that point in life if you haven't achieved true happiness beforehand. Part of the reason I feel so empty is because of how lucky I was before this tragic event. Millions of people search all their lives to find that one person they fit with, that they can share their life with. That one person with whom they can have their Jerry Maguire, you-complete-me life. And I did it, I found her. I literally accomplished that feat. I'd known Catherine for eighteen years. I'd lived with her for eleven years, and we'd been married for a wonderful seven years. She truly made me the person I am today. We shared everything together, and we were so happy. She also gave me two wonderful children, Declan and Violet, whom I will spend the rest of my life loving.

It's funny to realize that I wouldn't be so sad today if I wasn't once so happy to begin with. That's why sometimes I feel lucky, which is a strange and alien feeling to me at most times, but it also makes me smile. It makes me remember how wonderful our lives were together and that, for a brief moment in time, I had it all.

If you've made it this far, I do apologize. There's no secret, no magic potion, no pill, no one particular thing I can offer that can take away your pain if you have experienced your own tragedy, your own loss. But the one thing I can say is that you have to keep on living, you have to take care of yourself. You have to get up every morning and face the world. Trust me, I know it's hard as hell to do at times, but you have to do it. And surround yourself with family and friends, if you can, anybody who loves you, because you can't do it yourself. It's too much. The pain, the emptiness—it's too much of a burden to handle yourself. And lastly, remember that life is for the living, no matter how dark times may be, no matter how miserable you may feel. Never forget, life is for the living.

Online Guest Book from Catherine's Obituary Posting

October 24, 2012
Dearest Jerry and Barbara,
My heartfelt sympathies are with you and your family. I didn't know Catherine personally, but her father, Jerry, made me feel like she was a dear friend. May God guide you through your grievance with memories, prayers, family, and friends.

October 08, 2012
Gus,
My deepest sympathy to you and your loved ones. I pray for your peace, comfort, and understanding during this most difficult time. May God bless you and your children each and every day.

October 04, 2012
Gus,
I know I never met Catherine, but from the way you spoke of her, she sounded like an incredible woman. My thoughts and deepest sympathy go to you and your family.

October 04, 2012
Dear Jerry and Barbara,
Our prayers are with you, Catherine's children, and her husband and sister in this time of great loss and sorrow. We will always remember how wonderful she was and how you expressed such great pride in all she accomplished.

October 04, 2012
Dear Jerry and Barbara,
I will keep you and your family in my heart and prayers. I am so sorry for your loss. My love to you both.

October 04, 2012
Dr. Beck,
Words seem inadequate to help ease your loss. My thoughts and prayers of peace and comfort are with you and your family.

October 03, 2012
My thoughts and prayers are with the family. I took care of Declan and Violet at Rainbow. Catherine was a charming and beautiful person! We now have an angel waching over us all.

October 03, 2012
I worked for Catherine for a short period of time at Vorys, and I really enjoyed getting to know her. She will be missed. My thoughts and prayers will be with your family during this difficult time.

October 03, 2012
So very sorry to hear of Catherine's passing. I worked with her briefly in the B&F dept. at Ballard. Your family will be in my prayers.

October 03, 2012
With deepest sympathy.

October 03, 2012
There are no words to heal your loss at this time. Just know we are thinking about you and your family, and may God's love get you through this.

October 03, 2012
Dr. Beck and family,
So very sorry to hear of your loss. Remember all the good memories of your loved one. She will be your little angel in heaven.

October 03, 2012
Dr. Beck,
I am praying for you and your family during this most difficult time. Our Father in heaven will carry you through.

October 02, 2012
Dr. Beck,
My deepest sympathy. You are in my thoughts and prayers.

October 02, 2012
Dr. Beck,
My heart goes out to you and your family at this time of great loss. You are all in my thoughts and prayers. May all of your caring and compassion that you always give to others surround you and your family and hold you up in your time of need.

October 02, 2012
Dr. Beck,
I am so very sorry for your loss. My heart just breaks for you and your family. I pray for much peace for you and your family. May you find comfort in your happiest memories and the eyes of those beautiful babies. Please know you can always find lots of love and support from your Geauga family. Please let us know if there is anything we can do for any of you.

October 02, 2012
Jerry and Barbara,
Words can't express the sorrow we feel for your family. Just know you're in our thoughts and prayers. May God bless and comfort your family in this most difficult time.

October 02, 2012
Barbara and family,
Sending you love and strength as you grieve the loss of Catherine.

October 02, 2012
Dear family,
No words could ever express my deep-felt sorrow. Love you.

October 01, 2012
Hi Barbara,
Our heart goes out to you and your family. We are so very sorry to hear about the loss of your daughter Catherine. We are praying for you all. Love you.

October 01, 2012
Dr. Beck,
My heart aches for you and your family. You have my deepest sympathy. I think I speak for all of Geauga ICU nurses when I say that we love, respect, and care for you as a doctor...and even more so as a person. My prayers and thoughts for peace and healing to you, your babies, and your family. May God bless you.

October 01, 2012
Our prayers are with Catherine and all of her family. May she rest in peace. We knew Catherine to be a bright, friendly, and lovely girl at Lowden many years ago.

October 01, 2012
Gus,
I am shocked to hear this news. I send my sincerest sympathy to you, your babies, and all of the family. I went to Brush with Catherine and couldn't believe it when I saw the obituary in the paper. Sending many, many prayers and condolences to all of you.

October 01, 2012
Hi Dr. Beck,
I'm so sad to hear about your wife. Please know that I will pray for you and the babies.

October 01, 2012
We want to express our sympathy at the loss of Catherine. Know that you and your family are in our thoughts and prayers.

October 01, 2012
Gus,
My thoughts and prayers are with you and your family. Thinking of you.

October 01, 2012
So very sorry for your loss. My thoughts and prayers are with you all.

October 01, 2012
May time find you stronger each day as the love of friends and family surrounds you during this time of sadness.

October 01, 2012
Gus,
You and your family are in our prayers.

October 01, 2012
Dr. Beck,
My deepest sympathy goes out to you and your family. Thoughts and prayers for you and your babies.

October 01, 2012
My heart is so sad to hear this news. I went to Lowden with Catherine many moons ago. Prayers for peace and understanding that only the Lord can provide are sent out to the entire family.

October 01, 2012
May the Lord bless and comfort your family at this difficult time with his perfect peace, which passes all understanding.

October 01, 2012
My deepest sympathy for your great loss.

October 01, 2012
May the love of friends and family carry you through your grief.

October 01, 2012
May God bless you and your family in this time of sorrow.

October 01, 2012
Gus,
My family and I are thinking about you.

September 30, 2012
The family has lost a daughter, a wife, and a mother. We have lost a niece that will be remembered always. Catherine will be in our prayers as well as her loving family.

September 30, 2012
Condolences to the entire family. She will be missed.

September 30, 2012
My thoughts and prayers are with Catherine and her family during this very difficult time.

September 30, 2012
We'll hold Catherine in our hearts always as she lives on in the eyes of her babies.

September 30, 2012
May God hold you in the palm of his hand, dear Catherine.

Online Guest Book from Catherine's Funeral

Condolence:

Dear Gus,

My family and I are so very sorry for your loss. Let us know if we can help in any way. Our thoughts and prayers to you and your family.

Monday October 08, 2012

Condolence:

Gus,

We are incredibly sad to hear about your loss. Our deepest sympathies to you and your family. We are thinking of you and praying for you all. Your friends and colleagues from HUH.

Friday October 05, 2012

Condolence:

Dear Gus,

I am truly sorry for you and your family. No words can really help at this time, but know you and your wife's family are in our prayers.

Thursday October 04, 2012

Condolence:

Your family is in my thoughts and prayers. I worked with Catherine in Philadelphia— such a warm and generous person and great lawyer.

Wednesday October 03, 2012

Condolence:

Presently I realize that there is nothing I can say to you that will heal the wound in your heart. But please know that my heart and love is with you, and although today seems like too much to bear, remember she is a child of God and know that she will be remembered and loved. God be with you and your family at this time of mourning. You are always in my prayers.

Tuesday October 02, 2012

Condolence:
Dear Gus,
Thoughts and prayers to you and your family at this very difficult time.
So very sorry to hear of your loss.

Tuesday October 02, 2012

Condolence:
Dear Gus,
Words can't express how saddened we are to hear of your loss. Our
thoughts and prayers are with you and your family. Please let us know
if there is anything we can do.

Tuesday October 02, 2012

Condolence:
Barbara, Jerry, and loved ones,
Our hearts are broken with sadness at your loss. We are constantly
praying for and thinking of you all.

Tuesday October 02, 2012

Condolence:
Gus,
I am so sorry for your family's loss. I am praying for you and your fam-
ily. May God comfort and strengthen you during your time of need.

Tuesday October 02, 2012

Condolence:
I am so sorry to hear about your family's loss. I pray that healing, comfort, and peace will be with you. God bless you and your family during
this time of bereavement.

Monday October 01, 2012

Sundown
Sometimes I think it's a shame
When I get feelin' better when I'm feelin' no pain
(Gordon Lightfoot)

Made in the USA
Charleston, SC
20 February 2014